# FACING LIFE'S CHALLENGES HEAD ON

## HOW JESUS GETS YOU THROUGH WHAT YOU CAN'T GET AROUND

BOB JENNERICH

❀ Created with Vellum

# OTHER BOOKS BY THE AUTHOR

**Type this Url to Download My Free Ebook:**

https://dl.bookfunnel.com/usje1pnyu0

This Is God's Plan?! How We Can Be Certain in Days of Uncertainty

**Also available where books are sold**

God Is Everywhere! Recognizing Our Extraordinary God in Ordinary Life

*To God, who saved my life, and to Molly, Alli,
and Brian, who make it great*

# ACKNOWLEDGMENTS

Writing a book is far harder than I ever realized. I never would have been able to complete this project without so many people who helped make it a reality.

My incredible wife Molly has been listening to me talk about this book for two years. She has supported me with encouragement, by reading the manuscript several times, serving as its first editor, and making it far better than I had originally written it. I cannot possibly overestimate how amazing it has been to have her walk with me through this project, and through twenty-six years of marriage. All of my love.

My brother Steve Jennerich has been a great source of support. He's an author too, and we have been sharing our joys and struggles throughout the process. Until now, we had zero collective experience in writing a book and taking it to market. It's been fun to learn together and we've grown closer as brothers in Christ. I encourage you to check out his work. You can find him at BlueCollarMessenger.com.

I want to thank my parents, Walt and Joanne Jennerich, who have loved and supported me as parents do. They helped me finish the book and told me they were proud of me. What more could you ask of your parents? My brother-in-law Paul Weber has been a great friend throughout the process, reading, editing, and improving it with his suggestions.

The same could be said of my great friends Les Fleetwood, Matt Brant, and Larry Honea, who read the book, met with me either in person or over the phone, and gave valuable feedback that I incorporated into the book. Dr. Edwin Blum also read the original draft and helped me think through some of the theology of the book. Dr. Paul Pettit at my alma mater, Dallas Theological Seminary provided much needed advice about how to publish and market the book.

My two children, Allison and Brian have asked me about my progress on the book for two years now. You can't tell your kids you're writing a book and not finish it! I'm grateful for their love and support.

I owe a debt of gratitude to Jim Pence, my editor and friend. Jim caught factual mistakes in my original manuscript and helped with theology, flow, and vocabulary. Beyond that, Jim has been a valuable confidant and advisor to me as a first-time author, and answering my bottomless well of questions. It's one thing to write a first draft. Jim helped turn it into a book. If you're looking for an editor who goes above and beyond the call of duty, I recommend that you consider Jim. You can find him at JamesPence.com.

Hannah Linder designed the book cover. The first cover designer I hired was not quite able to capture what I wanted on the cover. Hannah nailed it on her first try. She's a talented graphic designer, book designer and author. I recommend that you look her up at HannahLinderDesigns.com.

I have been reading Joanna Penn's book series for self-published authors for the past several months. She has been a wealth of information and inspiration. If you are in the process of writing a book, you will find a ton of valuable advice at TheCreativePenn.com.

To you the reader, this is my first book. I am very grateful to you. The first time you read an unknown author, you don't know what to expect. You're taking a risk. The fact that you have trusted me with your money to buy the book and your time to read it means the world to me. I would love to know how you liked it.

If you enjoy this book think that others could benefit from it too, I would greatly appreciate a brief review. There is a link at the end of the book to do that. Reviews really help authors to help spread the word and to convince others that this book is worthy of their investment. Thank you for that.

You can connect with me on Facebook at Facebook.com/BobJennerich, and Twitter.com/bob_jennerich. Sign up for my email list to receive other free content on my website, BobJennerich.com. There you will also find a link to a 52-week devotional book called, "God is Everywhere!" You can also read my blog, and listen to my sermons delivered at Grace Redeemer Community Church, Garland, TX.

# CONTENTS

# INTRODUCTION

My wife's uncle Ken Weber died on December 18, 2002. Uncle Kenny's death marked the start of my journey to faith. It's the reason why I'm pastoring a church now, and why I wrote this book. I want to take a moment to honor both Uncle Kenny and God at the beginning of this book by telling you my story.

Before I became a pastor, I worked as a lawyer. That December, I was preparing for the biggest court trial of my career, and under crushing stress. Facing about thirty lawyers who were much more experienced and better financed than I was, I knew that I was outgunned and undermanned. I had just finished a deposition in preparation for the trial and decided to go see a movie to give myself a break. As soon as I sat down in the theater Molly called me, sobbing.

"Uncle Kenny had a massive heart attack," she finally managed. I left the theater and drove home to be with her. Uncle Kenny died a few days later.

I was raised in the Catholic church, but by the time I got to college, I was a full-blown atheist. College can shake your faith, but I abandoned mine on my own. I exchanged it for all the fun that college has to offer, and I didn't cheat myself out of any of it. Uncle Kenny's funeral changed everything.

It was a cold, rainy, miserable day. We stood by the graveside in the windswept rain, under umbrellas too small and puddles too big. Because Uncle Kenny had served and flew in the United States Air Force during the Vietnam War, he was honored with a military funeral. As the storm blew from every direction, the honor guard fired volleys from their rifles. They folded the flag and presented it to his wife, Molly's Aunt Joan.

Uncle Kenny's teenage children, Maggie and Michael, were completely devastated by the sudden loss of their father—their hero. I will always remember Michael—who had just been selected to attend the Air Force Academy exactly forty years after his own father—splayed out on top of the casket, sobbing uncontrollably.

As I saw their grief I thought, "If there is a God, why would He allow such pain and loss? Why would He allow Aunt Joan to be widowed so young and leave Maggie and Michael to grow up without their dad?"

The emotion of the funeral, the stress of my upcoming trial, and the sadness of Uncle Kenny's funeral overwhelmed me. I broke down in tears and couldn't stop crying. Molly and I missed half of the gathering back at their house after the funeral because I could not regain control of myself. After we returned, I looked around at people in Molly's family who I knew had faith. I could see that they had hope while all I felt was hopelessness. They believed that though Uncle Kenny was gone, they would see him again in heaven. I wanted that hope.

God used my own circumstances and Uncle Kenny's death to draw me to Him. After the funeral, I concluded that it was intellectually dishonest to call myself an atheist without ever truly investigating Christianity's claims. I decided to read the

Bible to see if there was any truth to the Christian faith and resolved to follow wherever the truth led, although I think in my heart of hearts I doubted that I would find Christianity's claims credible.

During the next two years, I read all of the New Testament. I read books about the reasons to believe in Christianity, such as *The Case for Christ*, by Lee Strobel, and *Evidence that Demands a Verdict*, by Josh McDowell. At some point during the next two years, the overwhelming weight of the evidence convinced me that Jesus Christ died, was buried, and was resurrected from the dead. I understood that He had to endure the cross to pay for my sins and that the proof that God accepted Jesus' payment for sin is that God raised Him from the dead. Because of Jesus' death and resurrection, I have eternal life. That's what it means to be a Christian, and I became one!

I was excited about my new faith. I wanted to immerse myself in ministry in some way, but without training or education, I couldn't even get an interview. In retrospect, I certainly understand. What church would hire a lawyer who's been a Christian for a month? I knew that if I were serious about being in ministry, I needed training. I also knew that I couldn't go to seminary and still afford the cost of living in New Jersey. So with my wife Molly's prayerful support, we decided that I would leave my law practice in New Jersey, that we would sell our house that had been in Molly's family for about 100 years, and move to Texas, so I could attend seminary. After four grueling, but blessed years, I graduated seminary, and now I'm the pastor of a church in North Texas. From atheist lawyer, to committed pastor; it's proof that all things are possible with God.

I wrote this book because I know first-hand that life is not easy. There are unexpected bumps all along the way, and I'll tell you about many of them in the chapters that follow. I have caused many of those bumps myself, either through ignorance, pride, lack of faith, failure to wait on God's timing, or any number of other reasons. I hope to show in this book that God is faithful even when we are not. Each chapter deals with a common source of life's struggles that I have battled against too. That's why I called the book, *Facing Life's Challenges Head On.* Life will knock us down from time to time, but knocked down doesn't have to mean knocked out. Learning to trust Jesus to help us get through what we can't get around increases our faith, and helps us learn that God loves us and that He's in control of our circumstances.

Uncle Kenny's death was tragic, but God used it. As an unbeliever, I didn't see how anything good could come from it. But something good did come from it. I'll be in heaven because God brought something good out of our family's tragedy. Death comes to us all. It truly is inevitable, but you can decide where you will spend eternity. Heaven awaits those who have trusted in Jesus Christ for their salvation. If you haven't done that yet, my hope is that you will. It's as simple as asking God to forgive your sins and telling Him that you trust in Jesus' death and resurrection alone for your salvation. Once you have done that, I pray that this book will encourage you to face life's challenges head on!

1

## ANXIETY

**"We were under great pressure, far beyond our ability to endure, so that we despaired of life itself." 2 Cor. 1:8-9**

I hesitate to write about anxiety. A few years ago it consumed me as you'll see from the story I'm about to tell you. I've learned to cope with it, but even today, just saying or writing the word makes me anxious as I think back on those days. Trying not to be anxious is like trying not to think about food when you're dieting. I'm not a psychiatrist or a psychologist. I recognize that anxiety and fear are like twins, similar yet different. I'm writing about them as a layperson using lay definitions and terminology. This is how I understand the difference between the two: Fear is a response to a real and present situation. Anxiety is a response to a potential situation that doesn't yet exist. It could happen, but it may never happen.

To say it another way, *Fear* results from a known or understood threat. *Anxiety* results from an unknown or poorly defined threat.[1] Fear is more of an acute response to a direct and immediate threat. Anxiety is more of a chronic, ever-present, butterflies in your stomach reaction to what could potentially happen.

To illustrate, if I were walking in the woods and came face to face with a bear, my natural response would be fear. If I have a doctor's appointment approaching, and I'm concerned about my health, my response would be anxiety. I'm aware that the lines between these two emotions are easily blurred. Anxiety can produce fear; fear can cause anxiety. Although it's impossible to completely separate anxiety from fear, this chapter focuses on the former. I'll have more to say about fear in the next chapter.

In the fall of 2014, I was just a couple of months from graduating from seminary. Throughout my studies, I had maintained my partnership in my law practice in New Jersey, but after we moved to Texas, it began to tank. We were not bringing in money. The firm was deep in debt, and I hadn't taken a paycheck in several months. Molly and I had spent all our personal savings and were starting to withdraw money from our retirement accounts to pay our monthly bills. We were under extreme financial pressure and considering bankruptcy.

I had been searching for a position in ministry but had no prospects. As graduation from seminary approached, I faced pressure to find a job and earn money. On top of that, I was working on a large case in New Jersey and made a significant mistake. Without boring you with a bunch of legal procedure, I missed an important deadline. The judge in the case refused to extend it and was forcing us to a trial for which we were unprepared. In addition to the other pressures, the possibility of a malpractice claim loomed. Then came the final straw.

. . .

IN NOVEMBER 2014 I TURNED IN THE LAST TWO PAPERS I WOULD ever write in seminary. I was so relieved to be done. About a week later, I received a voicemail from my professor saying that I cited my sources improperly, which equated to plagiarism under the seminary guidelines. He said seminary policy compelled him to fail me in the class and report me to the academic dean for further proceedings. That broke me. I can't describe how I felt. My blood ran cold, and I remember screaming out Molly's name for help. Wave after wave of *what-if* questions flooded my brain. What if the school expels me? What if I never graduate? What if no church will hire me and I have to find another job in the legal field to pay my bills?

I fell into a deep and dark depression with anxiety so severe that my body shook uncontrollably. I could barely get out of bed, move, or talk. I had no will to eat. I had virtually shut down. I even contemplated suicide. That's the power of anxiety. It's real, even if the things causing our anxiety never happen or are so far-fetched that they could never happen. In our own minds, our worst fears are not only possible, they become probable, and then they become inevitable. I call it *catastrophizing*. You get a paper cut, and you believe that you will get an incurable infection and die. No matter what the situation, your mind conceives the worst possible outcome, and you're convinced that it's going to happen. I have not yet defeated anxiety, but I have made meaningful progress. More about that later.

Once we recognize anxiety for what it is, a negative emotional response to a perceived threat, it is important to learn how to take healthy steps to control it. Otherwise, it can become a chronic problem with devastating effects. Let's look at a couple of Biblical heroes who faced anxiety to see what we can learn. Two Biblical stalwarts, Paul and David, show that even the best of us are subject to anxiety. First let's look at Paul.

CASE STUDY #1 - PAUL

Paul suffered from extreme anxiety at various points during his life as a Christian missionary. He traveled throughout the known world spreading the gospel of Jesus Christ. The problem was, the Jews considered Paul's teaching heretical because they thought he was preaching against the Law and Moses. As for the gentiles, the concept of one God was foreign, especially a God who would become human and die for the people's sins so that they might have eternal life.

Paul explained it like this, "For indeed Jews ask for signs and Greeks search for wisdom; but we preach Christ crucified, to Jews a stumbling block and to Gentiles foolishness" (1 Cor. 1:22-23). Paul suffered severe persecution from both Jews and Greeks due to his unpopular message.

Paul wrote 2 Corinthians during his second missionary journey which took him from Asia to Greece and back again. Something very traumatic must have happened to Paul during his time in Asia. This is what he wrote to the Corinthians: "We do not want you to be uninformed, brothers and sisters, about the troubles we experienced in the province of Asia. We were under great pressure, far beyond our ability to endure, so that we despaired of life itself. Indeed, we felt we had received the sentence of death (2 Cor. 1:8).

We don't know precisely which of Paul's sufferings he was referring to here. However, later in the letter, Paul summarized his experiences up to that point. In Chapter 11, Paul wrote:

I was beaten times without number, often in danger of death. Five times I received from the Jews thirty-nine lashes. Three times I was beaten with rods, once I was stoned, three times I was shipwrecked, a night and a day I have spent in the deep. I have been on frequent journeys, in dangers from rivers, dangers from robbers, dangers from my countrymen, dangers from the Gentiles, dangers in the city, dangers in the wilderness, dangers on the sea, dangers among false brethren; I have been in labor and hardship, through many sleepless nights, in hunger and thirst, often without food, in cold and exposure. Apart from *such* external things, there is the daily pressure on me *of* concern for all the churches. Who is weak without my being weak? Who is led into sin without my intense concern? (2 Cor. 11:23-29).

Much of the suffering Paul described was physical. But he was also under significant emotional pressure. The suffering Paul described in 2 Corinthians 1 was worse than any of the physical torture he wrote about in chapter 11. Listen to the raw emotion in Paul's writing: "We were under great pressure, far beyond our ability to endure, so that we despaired of life itself. Indeed, we felt we had received the sentence of death." Paul was in agony, unable to escape the anxiety of what he thought might happen to him. The word despair denotes hopelessness. John Calvin translated the Greek word for despair as "trembling anxiety. [2]

The text says not that they had *received* the sentence of death, but that they *felt they had received* the sentence of death. Whatever the circumstances may have been, Paul allowed his anxiety to control his thoughts. He catastrophized the situation so that in his imagination, whatever had happened led all the way to the worst possible outcome. Paul was quite sure he was about to die for the sake of the gospel. Why did God allow this?

## God Uses Anxiety to Strengthen Us

Somehow Paul escaped the sentence of death that he believed was on him. This was a significant learning experience for Paul about how to deal with the fears and anxiety that would accompany him throughout his ministry. Paul shared with the Corinthians what he learned from this experience of anxiety. At some point, the suffering had ended. The threat was over. Paul was able to reflect on it with the benefit of greater spiritual maturity. While in the thick of it, Paul felt like the sentence of death was on him, but once it was over he understood that God had a purpose in suffering, so he could say in the second half of verse 9, "But this happened that we might not rely on ourselves but on God, who raises the dead" (2 Cor. 1:9 NIV).

When trouble comes, and we find ourselves under a tremendous burden, we tend to focus on ourselves and our problems. When it happened to me, I was so overwhelmed by the pressure, that I could barely pray or even think about God. I couldn't consider how God could use my problems for any worthwhile purpose. I allowed my mind to spin, moving from problem to catastrophe, asking what-if questions and convincing myself that the worst possible outcome was the only possible outcome.

Anxiety is a real mental illness. People who experience it often need medical treatment, as I did. But I believe that part of the reason it reaches such a deep level is that we try to solve problems that only the Lord can resolve. Without God, we dig our hole deeper, which leads to further despair and anxiety.

Paul teaches us that greater spiritual maturity leads to stronger reliance on God.

God allows trouble so that we will come to trust Him and depend on Him more than we ever have before. Paul learned to trust the Lord with every threat and problem he faced. It's a stunning statement that Paul made: "This happened that we might not rely on ourselves but on God who raises the dead." How foolish of us to rely on ourselves to fix a problem when we can rely on God who has the power to raise the dead!

Jesus said it so perfectly: "And which of you by worrying can add a *single* hour to his life's span? If then you cannot do *even a very little thing*, why do you worry about other matters" (Luke 12:25-26, emphasis added). Can you imagine calling it a "very little thing" to add an hour to our lives? God wants us to depend on Him for all things. He allows trouble to strengthen our faith and teach us that He is the solution to our problems.

Over time, our confidence in God will continue to grow, as Paul's did. Paul knew that fresh troubles would come, but now armed with the knowledge that God is powerful to rescue, he could say: "He has delivered us from such a deadly peril, and he will deliver us again. On him we have set our hope that he will continue to deliver us" (2 Cor. 1:10 NIV). Since God had saved him from his past trials, Paul was confident that God would protect him in the future.

Paul wrote 2 Corinthians near the time of the riot in the temple of Artemis in Ephesus described in Acts 19. The events of Acts 20-28 hadn't happened yet. Paul's journey to Jerusalem, where the Jews would beat him and might have murdered him if the Roman centurion hadn't intervened, still lay ahead of him. He still had a two-year imprisonment in Caesarea and two imprisonments in Rome to look forward to. Nero would execute him in Rome years later.

Paul didn't know any of these things when he wrote 2 Corinthians. All he knew was that God had been faithful to him in the past, and that he could trust God to remain faithful in the future. Whenever you see a commercial on TV for some investment, there is always a disclaimer that says something like, "Past performance is not always indicative of future earnings." That's because the stock market is volatile and unpredictable. But God never needs a disclaimer because He is unchanging and trustworthy. That's why Paul set his hope on God. The Greek word *hope* does not mean crossing your fingers and hoping rain doesn't wash out your weekend barbeque. Biblical hope is expectation of what is sure, what is certain to happen, based on who God is and the assurance of His promises. Paul could face whatever was next because God had strengthened him. But God also uses all hardships, even anxiety, to strengthen others.

### GOD USES ANXIETY TO STRENGTHEN OTHERS

Paul said in verse 8, "we do not want you to be unaware." He knew that honestly sharing his sufferings and God's deliverance would strengthen the Corinthians' faith. It would give them hope that God would deliver them from their troubles as well. Paul's transparency and authenticity is one of the many ways he made disciples.

In verse 11, Paul continued that theme. God will "continue to deliver us as you help us by your prayers" (2 Cor. 1:11 NIV). Paul was constantly asking for prayer in his letters because God works through the prayers of His people. Many would give thanks because God answered their prayers. Has anyone ever said to you, "God never gives you more than you can bear?" Don't you hate that? That's because it's not true. Sometimes,

God gives us *far more* than we can bear *so that,* by our prayer and the prayer of others, we will rely on Him only, *so that* when God delivers us, we will be comforted. With stronger faith, we can comfort others when they are going through their own trials. That's the cycle of discipleship. We learn to trust in God through trouble and sometimes anxiety, as He delivers us from them. God allows individuals to suffer so the whole body may grow into spiritual maturity. In Ephesians Paul described the church as "citizens being fitted together...growing into a holy temple in the Lord" (Eph. 2:21). It is God's will for us to grow spiritually as individuals, but it is also His will that we grow spiritually as a body.

Anxiety festers when we think we are alone in it. We may begin to believe that God has forgotten us or doesn't care. We may even feel like we "have received the sentence of death." We lack the hope that God will deliver us. Sometimes we feel like God doesn't know or care about our suffering. He does know about it, of course, but maybe God's purpose in our suffering is for us to share it with others, so that others will share in the blessing that will come when He delivers us. When God's people unite in prayer and He answers, everyone rejoices. When we struggle together, we grow in spiritual maturity together. King David is a good example of this.

CASE STUDY #2 – DAVID

We don't know why David wrote Psalm 55, but it may have been in response to his friend Ahithophel's treachery during the rebellion of David's son Absalom. Whatever the reason, David wrote Psalm 55 out of extreme anxiety. Consider his words because of this betrayal:

Give ear to my prayer, O God; And do not hide Yourself from my supplication. Give heed to me and answer me; I am restless in my complaint and am surely distracted, Because of the voice of the enemy, Because of the pressure of the wicked; For they bring down trouble upon me, And in anger they bear a grudge against me. My heart is in anguish within me, And the terrors of death have fallen upon me. Fear and trembling come upon me, And horror has overwhelmed me. I said, "Oh, that I had wings like a dove! I would fly away and be at rest" (Psalm 55:1-6 NIV).

David's life was in danger because his close friend had betrayed him, and David lamented over the betrayal.

"For it is not an enemy who reproaches me, Then I could bear *it*; Nor is it one who hates me who has exalted himself against me, Then I could hide myself from him. But it is you, a man my equal, my companion and my familiar friend; We who had sweet fellowship together, Walked in the house of God in the throng" (Psalm 55:12-14 NIV).

Betrayal is always terrible, but when it comes from someone you love, and who you thought loved you, it is especially unbearable. Like when your best friend steals your girlfriend or boyfriend. There are unwritten rules that friends should not break. David prayed in his distress that death would come upon his betrayers. But for him personally, he had two remedies.

Remedy #1 – Call Upon the Lord

David's first remedy was to call upon the Lord. He had complete confidence in the Lord that He would save him.

As for me, **I shall call upon God** and the Lord will save me. Evening and morning and at noon, I will complain and murmur, And He will hear my voice. He will redeem my soul in peace from the battle *which is* against me, For they are many *who strive* with me. God will hear and answer them- Even the one who sits enthroned from of old; With whom there is no change, and who do not fear God (Psalm 55:16-19 emphasis added).

It's always a good start to call upon the Lord, rather than to try to fix problems in our own power. David had complete confidence in God. What was David's second remedy?

REMEDY #2 – CAST YOUR BURDEN ON THE LORD

David used a two-part process to relieve his anxiety. First, he called on the Lord, then he cast his burden on the Lord. "*Cast your burden on the Lord* and he will sustain you. He will never allow the righteous to be shaken" (Psalm 55:22).

David was more able to relax because of these two actions. God would not allow the righteous to be shaken. David allowed God to handle the situation rather than trying to overcome it in his own power. Sometimes we make our problems so much worse by trying to fix them ourselves rather than allowing God to do the work. David called on the Lord and cast his burden on Him, and recorded the result in verse 23: "You, O God, will bring them down to the pit of destruction; Men of bloodshed and deceit will not live out half their days. But I will trust in You."

It's so freeing to leave our problems with God and to allow Him to deal with them. But how often we go back and pick them up again. David did not do this. He left his difficulties with the Lord and trusted in Him. His anxiety was gone.

## HOW DO WE MANAGE OUR ANXIETY?

What have we learned so far? From David, to call on the Lord and cast our cares on Him. From Paul, that God's purpose in our anxiety is to strengthen our faith, so we can strengthen the faith of others. Here are a few other things we can do:

### DON'T CATASTROPHIZE THE PROBLEM

Paul wrote in Romans 12 that we should judge ourselves with "sober judgment." Sober means to be able to think in a sound or rational manner, to judge ourselves correctly. The same surely applies to our problems. Judge them accurately. Evaluate them properly. Ask yourself if this situation will matter in one month, one year, or five years. Don't imagine your circumstances to be worse than they truly are. In other words, don't catastrophize! If we can do this, it will help to manage anxiety.

### PRAY FOR OTHERS

Anxiety causes us to turn inward. We focus so much on ourselves and our problems that there is no room for God or others. Develop the discipline of praying for others. Here's a suggestion: Draw a six-ringed target on a piece of paper. Your family is the bullseye. The next ring is for people in your church. The next ring could include people at your job. Reserve the next ring for people in the church worldwide. In the next ring, put our country and its leaders and its issues. In the outmost ring include unbelieving friends and neighbors. Then pray through the target from the bullseye outward. Then, pray it again in reverse. Be creative. Nothing helps to take your mind off yourself and your problems like focusing on God and His love and praying for others.

When you pray for others, you'll also find yourself prepared to serve them. You'll realize that their challenges are as difficult as your own, and your focus will be re-directed from yourself to others, and your anxiety will decrease.

### PRACTICE AN ATTITUDE OF GRATITUDE

Another way to decrease anxiety is to continually list the things that you are grateful for and thank God for them. We tend to focus on the one thing that is wrong in our lives and not the many things that God has so graciously provided. Keep a list of answered prayers so you can remember God's faithfulness. The old song is true: "Count your blessings, name them one by one. Count your many blessings, see what God has done."[3]

## CONCLUSION

I want to be as genuine as I can be with you here. I don't want to portray myself as some super-spiritual Christian, cured by only immersing myself deeper into the word of God and relying solely on Him. That's not how it happened. I desperately needed the word of God, and I clung to it as best as I could, but I needed more. I needed to see a psychologist to learn coping strategies, and a psychiatrist who could prescribe medication. I needed Molly desperately. I wouldn't let her out of my sight for even a minute. I don't know why, but I felt like I was safer if I could see her. Imagine how draining that must have been for her.

One of the things we did together during this time was to go out for praise walks. It was the winter of 2014-15, a frigid winter by Texas standards, and Molly hates the cold. But she went out with me every day because it helped me. We tried to cast our burdens on the Lord while walking. We would walk and take turns praising God for our marriage, our kids, our house, our physical health, the beautiful sky, whatever we could think of. We would pray the attributes of God by the first letter of the attribute. She would pray, "God you are awesome." I would pray, "God you are beautiful, etc.," all the way through the alphabet. We would list the things we were thankful for. We would pray for others. Some days I could participate. Most days were so bad that I could only listen to her pray. We would listen to sermons while we did jigsaw puzzles at the dining room table. I wrote encouraging Bible verses on sticky notes and stuck them around the edges of my computer monitor.

Mornings were the worst. I would wake up shaking like a leaf. I'd take my anxiety medicine and start counting the minutes until I could take another dose. The way my brain's chemistry worked, I tended to feel better at night. Some nights I felt like I might even be okay. But in the morning, the cycle would begin again. It was like the movie *Groundhog Day*. Even if I felt a little better at night, I dreaded going to sleep because I knew my anxiety would be back full throttle in the morning. This continued for many months.

One Sunday at Stonebriar Community Church, Steve Farrar preached a message from Psalm 71. He finished his sermon by quoting "For Your righteousness, O God, *reaches* to the heavens, You who have done great things; O God, who is like You? *You who have shown me many troubles and distresses will revive me again"* (Psalm 71:19-20 NASB1995, emphasis added). Molly and I looked at each other and fell into each other's arms crying, right there in the church service with 2000 people present. It was a stirring and moving moment I will always remember as we hoped and prayed that we could trust God's promise to revive us again.

I wish I could say that the word of God pulled me out of it. It helped, but it wasn't enough. My escape from anxiety came from a combination of several things. First, Molly had an anxiety crisis of her own, caused by the unrelenting stress of dealing with me. She had been so strong for so long, but the burden of caring for me was too much. Once we were both dealing with it, her need for care gave me purpose, and contributed to me emerging from my own anxiety. Another contributing factor was that I began work in Dallas as a contract attorney on a temporary basis. Suddenly I had reasons to get out of bed again: to care for Molly and to earn money, and we were able to slowly get our noses above water financially.

God addressed my other problems too. My partner was able to settle the case that I mentioned to our client's satisfaction, so the threat of the malpractice claim against us was resolved. Finally, on the plagiarism issue, I wasn't present for the meetings, but it seems that my professor conferred with the seminary, and they decided that my citing sources improperly was not intentional or egregious. My professor gave me a passing grade, and I graduated on schedule. Those things, combined with medication and a heavy reliance on the word of God and prayer, eventually brought me out of my crisis.

In December 2016, we were finally able to pay the debts of the law firm and close it. In January 2017, I answered an ad for a pastoral position. Soon after, I began interviewing for the role

I now hold as pastor at Grace Redeemer Community Church in Garland, Texas. I praise the Lord often for leading me out of darkness and back into the light. It didn't happen as quickly as I wanted it to, but the Lord did revive me again, and he revived Molly too. We both continue to take mild doses of anti-anxiety medication when needed. We have learned not to fool around with anxiety. We recognize how destructive it is, and our need to manage it.

I learned several lessons during this period of my life that I want to share with you, like Paul shared his with the Corinthians.

**1. I am so weak.** I had never considered myself a fragile person. But anxiety taught me that in the right (or wrong) circumstances, I am completely helpless. Anxiety broke my mind. It crushed my pride. I never thought that anything could cause me to think about suicide, but the longer the anxiety went on, the more my thoughts turned from, "Should I do it?" to, "How can I do it painlessly, and without my wife or kids finding me?" Those thoughts shattered all delusions of self-sufficiency and strength. That was an incredibly humbling and important lesson to learn.

**2. I love my wife.** I always knew that I was in love with my wife. But watching her stand by my side and care for me as I suffered through this, spending every waking minute with me to try to help me, cemented our love. As I watched her go through her own struggle, I was able to return the care that she had given to me. It has strengthened our relationship and made it stronger than it ever was.

**3. I need other believers, and they need me.** I am an introvert by nature. Most times I am happy alone in my office studying or reading. Anxiety taught me that I needed other believers. Several invested in me during this time. They invited me out to dinner, which blessed Molly as much as me. She needed a break, and I needed other believers to speak into my life and encourage me. I had a group of friends who would take me out to dinner, and then we would pray in one of their cars, which we called the prayer-mobile. I called a few other friends on the phone and was buoyed by their support. I relied on those friendships and time spent with other believers in my church. They helped me immensely during those difficulties.

Once the crisis was over, we were able to bless all the people who were praying for us. Just like Paul did with the Corinthians, when we shared our story with others, they received a blessing, and their faith was strengthened. Since then, we have been able to encourage many others who were suffering with anxiety or depression.

**4. I needed more compassion and empathy.** People hire an attorney to make them financially whole. A pastor's job is to help people become spiritually whole. I was not prepared to do that before my crisis. In seminary, I learned a lot about the Bible. I learned basic Hebrew and Greek. But seminary can't teach you compassion for people. It can't teach you to feel their pain and be willing to help. That can only come from a change to your heart and soul. Before my anxiety crisis, I would minimize or even mock other people's problems. I'd think, "Why can't you just make yourself happy? Go get an ice cream and cheer up." I had no empathy or compassion for people. Molly wasn't sure I was cut out to be a pastor. She used to pray, "God, if you're going to make him a pastor, give him a pastor's heart." God used anxiety to do it. It was only after I had experienced it, that I understood that people can't make themselves happy, and it's not shameful.

We are all broken people. When my anxiety was severe, the things that I worried about might have seemed silly to anyone else. But to me they were as real as a grizzly bear. Before I could be an effective pastor, I needed to learn that other people were the same. Although I might not understand their anxiety, it was as real to them as can be. God taught me never to minimize anyone else's problems, but to have empathy and compassion.

**5. You can't minister to others when you're broken.** Before God allowed anxiety to crush me, I was nowhere near prepared to be a pastor. God used it to prepare me for the role that he had for me. During my crisis, I was frustrated because I was applying for pastoral positions but receiving very few interviews. Now I know why. I was unprepared to help others because of my own brokenness. I would never want to suffer severe anxiety again, but I know that God allowed it, and used it for His purposes to prepare me for what He had for me to do. Now I am grateful for it. Just like Paul and David, God strengthened me through anxiety so I could empower others. Now I understand what James meant when he said, "Consider it all joy when you go through troubles of many kinds" (James 1:2). We don't rejoice in the trouble, but we rejoice in its results. God receives all praise and glory for using a very difficult experience to prepare me for the work of shepherding and caring for His flock. He will do the same for you.

Read the beautiful words of William Cowper in his hymn, "God Moves in a Mysterious Way":

> God moves in a mysterious way
> His wonders to perform;
> He plants His footsteps in the sea
> And rides upon the storm.
>
> Deep in unfathomable mines
> Of never-failing skill

He treasures up His bright designs
And works His sov'reign will

Ye fearful saints, fresh courage take;
The clouds ye so much dread
Are big with mercy and shall break
In blessings on your head.

Judge not the Lord by feeble sense,
But trust Him for His grace;
Behind a frowning providence
He hides a smiling face.

His purposes will ripen fast,
Unfolding every hour;
The bud may have a bitter taste,
But sweet will be the flow'r.

Blind unbelief is sure to err
And scan His work in vain;
God is His own interpreter,
And He will make it plain. [4]

# 2

# FEAR

"Do not fear, for I am with you; Do not anxiously look about you, for I am your God. I will strengthen you, surely I will help you, Surely I will uphold you with My righteous right hand." Isaiah 41:10

Before I became a pastor, I practiced law for about twenty years. I didn't like it very much, and the worst thing for me was when I had to take a case to trial. Mercifully, those were rare since parties usually settle their disputes before trial. Jury trials terrified me.

In the previous chapter, I sketched my understanding of the difference between fear and anxiety. Fear is a response to an existing situation or stimulus. Anxiety is a response to a situation that doesn't yet exist but could potentially exist. There is a fine line between the two, and certainly some overlap. My response to jury trials was fear because I believed I knew what *would* happen rather than what *might* happen. I feared losing the case or being publicly humiliated in front of the jury or my client if I got out-lawyered. I was afraid of not being properly prepared, of not knowing what to do or say if something unexpected happened. All these fears gripped me and controlled me to the point that I couldn't eat, sleep, or otherwise function. Some lawyers project supreme confidence in their abilities and the merits of their case. I worked hard to hide my fear and look confident, but I'm not sure I fooled anyone.

In December 2002, I represented a newly built condominium association in a case against the builder of their complex for substandard work, materials, and for taking short cuts from the original building plans. The builder then sued about thirty of its subcontractors, alleging that if there were deficiencies, the subcontractors were responsible. Suddenly, nearly three dozen lawyers joined ranks against me. I can't adequately convey the fear that gripped me as an under-experienced trial lawyer going to battle against a host of very experienced lawyers. The court scheduled our case for trial in early December 2002. This is the trial that I was talking about in the Introduction to this book. The process for this type of litigation is that the parties appear in court on the day of trial before a judge known as the assignment judge, whose job it is to assign your case to any available trial judge.

On our scheduled day, no judges were available, so the assignment judge told us to come back tomorrow. The same thing happened the next day, and the day after. This went on every day into January. We'd show up in court and hear, "No judges available today. Come back tomorrow."

Every time the assignment judge said, "No judges available today," I felt like I'd received a stay of execution. I was momentarily relieved of my fear that my trial would begin in the next half hour. But when the judge said, "Come back tomorrow," all that fear came flooding back. One of those days, a trial judge would surely be available. It was only a matter of time before I would have to face a jury and a huge team of high-priced lawyers. My client's board of directors had a dollar amount that they were willing to accept to settle the case, but when all the various defendant's offers were added up, the total didn't approach that number. A trial was all but inevitable. Fear, more like, abject terror filled my heart and ruined my Christmas that year. All of this was a major contributing factor to my breakdown during Molly's uncle Kenny's funeral that started me on my faith journey.

## FEAR DEFINED

The word *fear* as used in the Bible has two meanings. The first is how we would normally use the word in English. It refers to an emotional and physiological response to a threat. It can be an immediate threat, for example, "As Pharaoh drew near, the sons of Israel looked, and behold, the Egyptians were marching after them, and *they became very frightened*; so the sons of Israel cried out to the Lord" (Exodus 14:10 emphasis added). Fear can also be a threat of what will happen tomorrow or in the more distant future. Jacob had stolen his brother Esau's blessing many years earlier, but when he learned that Esau was on his way to meet him, Jacob feared for his life.

The messengers returned to Jacob, saying,

> "We came to your brother Esau, and furthermore he is coming to meet you, and four hundred men are with him." Then Jacob was greatly afraid and distressed; and he divided the people who were with him, and the flocks and the herds and the camels, into two companies; for he said, "If Esau comes to the

one company and attacks it, then the company which is left will escape" (Gen. 32:6-8).

Both the threat of Pharaoh coming on the Israelites and Esau coming to meet Jacob produced genuine fear. The only difference was in the immediacy of the danger.

The second way the Bible uses the word fear is in the sense of having a profound measure of respect, reverence, or awe of God. When we read verses like "*The fear of the Lord* is the beginning of knowledge" (Proverbs 1:7), it is this second sense of the word fear that is meant. A better translation of the verse might be, "The reverent awe of the Lord is the beginning of knowledge." Once we truly understand who God is and who we are by comparison, and we hold Him in reverent awe, then we can begin to be wise. Without this understanding, we cannot hope to be wise.

Fear, the emotional and physiological response to a real threat, can be good. When the threat is immediate it produces a flight or fight response, which can save our lives. But when the stimulus is not immediate, fear can be a debilitating emotion that can paralyze us into inaction. Fear of tomorrow ruins today. It puts a chokehold on every blessing today might bring (see Matthew 6:34).

The way to conquer fear in the first sense (an emotional and physiological response to a threat) is to train ourselves to replace it with reverent awe and trust in God. Obviously, I'm not talking about the kind of fear we experience when we come face to face with a grizzly bear. I'm talking about actual fear, but when the threat is less immediate, like Jacob's fear of his brother Esau, or when the threat is even less immediate or well-defined, such as my fear of jury trials. In that case, a proper reverent awe of God will lead to increased faith. If we understand His love for us, and His goodness and sovereignty, and intentionally redirect our focus on those attributes of God, we will have less fear. God loves us (John 3:16). God is in control (Isaiah 45:7). Nothing can happen to us that God doesn't allow for His sovereign purposes (Romans 8:28). It's not that we need to have *more* faith. The Bible says that if we have faith the size of a mustard seed we can move mountains. It's that we need to redirect our focus away from the source of our fear and toward God, the object of our faith.

## THE SOURCE OF FEAR

Where does fear come from? Why does it reign over our lives? Fear is often a combination of believing a lie from Satan and forgetting God's promises. Believing Satan's lies turns us away from trust in God and toward fear of the future. The issue in dealing with fear is whether we choose to believe God's promises or Satan's lies. James says that in God, "there is no variation or *shifting* shadow (James 1:17, emphasis added). John adds, "Your word is truth" (John 17:17). The author of Hebrews wrote, "Jesus Christ is the same yesterday and today and forever" (Hebrews 13:8). God is truth. He does not lie. He cannot lie (Hebrews 6:18) because it is against His nature to do so.

The Bible tells us over and over that God loves us, that He is good (Ps. 34:8), merciful (Eph. 2:4), and has plans for us (Jer. 29:11; Proverbs 16:9). On the other hand, Jesus said that Satan, "... was a murderer from the beginning and does not stand in the truth because there is no truth in him. Whenever he speaks a lie, he speaks from his own nature, for he is a liar and the father of lies" (John 8:44). If that's the case, why would we ever choose to believe Satan rather than God?

When we face challenging times, we want God to do something as quickly as possible. As we mature in our faith, we come to understand that when God doesn't intervene as quickly as we would like, it's because He has something to teach us in this hardship. He has something better for us than what we are praying for. Tim Keller wrote, "God will either give us what we ask or give us what we would have asked if we knew everything he knows."[1]

We know theologically that God loves us, that Jesus died for us, and that He wants the best for us. The hard part is to apply our knowledge practically, rather than just knowing it theoretically. It can be hard to weather the storm and wait on God and His timing.

Satan is not all-knowing but knows from observation where we are weak. He knows the mistakes we make and the guilt we carry. He knows that we have fears and preys upon our apprehension of the future. When God doesn't give us what we ask for, Satan and his demons are right there telling us that God doesn't love us, that we don't deserve answered prayer because of our sin, that we are not worthy of God's time and effort and on and on. When we don't trust God, we are choosing to believe Satan's lies whether we know it or not.

What happens when we believe the lie? We feel like we are adrift at sea, floating in uncertainty because we have become untethered from God who loves us. Without God as our anchor, our faith weakens, and Satan's deception stimulates all-consuming, fearful thoughts. The more we focus on God's promises and His faithfulness, the less we will fear the future. The best indicator of future performance is past performance. Even though God has delivered us from trial after trial, sometimes we still forget that what He has done in the past is the best predictor of what He will do in the future. Some of the most famous Biblical characters did this too, even after great blessing.

## BIBLICAL EXAMPLES OF FEAR

We can learn lessons from these three Biblical personalities.

### ELIJAH

In 1 Kings 18, Elijah won a great victory over the prophets of Baal, but suddenly became terrified of Jezebel's threat to kill him.

> Now Ahab told Jezebel all that Elijah had done, and how he had killed all the prophets with the sword. Then Jezebel sent a messenger to Elijah, saying, "So may the gods do to me and even more, if I do not make your life as the life of one of them *by tomorrow about this time.*" And *he was afraid and arose and ran for his life* and came to Beersheba, which belongs to Judah, and left his servant there. But he himself went a day's journey into the wilderness, and came and sat down under a juniper tree; and he requested for himself that he might die, and said, "It is enough; now, O Lord, take my life, for I am not better than my fathers (1 Kings 19:1-4 emphasis added).

What happened? Elijah had just watched God incinerate his saturated sacrifice with fire from heaven and allowed him to kill the prophets of Baal with the sword. Now he's afraid of the threat of one woman? It's hard to tell from the Biblical narrative what Elijah was thinking. Somehow, between verses two and three, Elijah lost his focus on God. He forgot what God had just done at Mount Carmel. Instead, he fixated on Jezebel, the object of his fear, rather than God who had just sent fire from the sky. He feared for his life and fled to escape Jezebel rather than trusting God to protect him. God came to Elijah there. He encouraged him and told him not to fear. Later He told Elijah that the dogs would eat Jezebel (1 Kings 21:23). The Lord strengthened Elijah. It was only when Elijah remembered the Lord and refocused his attention on Him, that he had the courage to overcome his fears.

### GIDEON

There is a repeated pattern in the Book of Judges. The people of Israel fall into sin. As punishment, God allows a foreign nation to take Israel captive. Israel cries out for deliverance. God raises up a military leader, called a judge, who defeats Israel's enemies and sets them free. Then, the people of Israel return to their sin. God again allows enemies to take Israel captive, and the cycle repeats.

In one episode, the Midianites had ruled over Israel for seven years. When Israel cried out for deliverance, God heard and raised up Gideon as a judge. Judges 6-7 tells his story.

> The angel of the Lord appeared to [Gideon] and said, "The Lord is with you, O valiant warrior." Then Gideon said to him, "O my lord, if the Lord is with us, why then has all this happened to us? And where are all His miracles which our fathers told us about, saying, 'Did not the Lord bring us up from Egypt?' But now the Lord has abandoned us and given us into the hand of Midian" (Judges 6:12-13).

Gideon's faith wavered. He focused on his enemies rather than God. Maybe he thought God was punishing him for something. His reaction is telling. *Why has all this happened to us? Where are all His miracles? Now the Lord has abandoned us.*

The angel of the Lord commanded Gideon to deliver Israel from the Midianites because the Lord would be with him. Instead, Gideon demanded a sign. He asked the angel to wait while he prepared a sacrifice. The angel of the Lord burned up his offering with his staff to prove to him that he could trust his message. But when Gideon realized he had seen God face to face he became afraid that he would die. The angel had to reassure him that he would not die. Later that same night, the Lord commanded Gideon to destroy his father's idols. He obeyed but did it at night because he was afraid. Ironically, his father, an idol worshipper, protected Gideon from the wrath of the men of the city.

After this, the Spirit of the Lord came upon Gideon to lead the Israelites against the Midianites and Amalekites. But Gideon was still afraid. In fear and doubt, Gideon asked for confirmation of his calling. He put out a wool fleece on the ground and asked God to make the fleece wet with dew while the ground remained dry as a sign that God was with Him. When God did as Gideon asked, he tested Him again. He asked this time for the ground to be wet with dew and keep the fleece dry. And it happened as he had asked. Then the Lord commanded Gideon to go up and fight the Midianites with only 300 men. God said, "If you are afraid to go down, go with Purah your servant down to the camp, and you will hear what they say; and afterward your hands will be strengthened that you may go down against the camp." Gideon was still afraid, because the text says, "he went with Purah his servant down to the outposts of the army that was in the camp" (Judges 7:10-11).

That night, Gideon overheard the Midianites discussing a dream of how God had given them into Gideon's hands. Finally,

Gideon gained confidence. He overcame his many apprehensions. He understood that God had already granted the victory. He kept his eyes on God's promises rather than his own fears. And not long after that, "When they blew 300 trumpets, the Lord set the sword of one against another even throughout the whole army; and the army fled as far as Beth-shittah toward Zererah, as far as the edge of Abel-meholah, by Tabbath" (Judges 7:22). God won the victory Himself. All Gideon had to do was to blow the trumpet.

## SAUL

Samuel was the last judge of Israel. The people of Israel were tired of judges. They wanted a king like the other nations and they demanded that Samuel give them one. Samuel lamented their plea but approached God with their request. God said, "Listen to the voice of the people in regard to all that they say to you, for they have not rejected you, but they have rejected Me from being king over them" (1 Sam. 8:7). The people wanted a man to lead them. God chose Saul, a man who appeared fit to be king. He was tall and handsome, a mighty man of valor. His problem was that he had a spirit of fear, and it plagued him his entire life.

When it was time for Saul's coronation, he hid among the baggage because of his fear. The people found him and crowned him king anyway. Saul won several battles in his early years, and God proved several times that He was with him. That should have increased Saul's faith, but 1 Samuel 13 tells us that Saul's spirit of fear overtook him again. The Philistines assembled against Saul at Gilgal, but Saul was afraid because his army was outnumbered by more than ten to one, and his own people were deserting him. Saul panicked.

It was customary to offer a burnt offering to the Lord as an act of prayer and worship before combat. Such offerings were to be conducted by priests such as Samuel, not kings. But the battle was about to start and Samuel was not there. Outnumbered and afraid, Saul offered the sacrifice. As soon as he finished, Samuel arrived.

> Samuel said to Saul, "You have acted foolishly; you have not kept the commandment of the Lord your God, which He commanded you, for now the Lord would have established your kingdom over Israel forever. But now your kingdom shall not endure. The Lord has sought out for Himself a man after His own heart, and the Lord has appointed him as ruler over His people, because you have not kept what the Lord commanded you" (1 Sam. 13:13-14).

Saul had been victorious in battle many times before, but he never learned to re-direct his focus to God when he faced fear. It cost him the kingdom that God had given to him.

In confronting Saul, Samuel got to the heart of the problem. He asked, "Is it not true, though *you were little in your own eyes*, you were made head of the tribes of Israel?" (1 Sam. 15:17 emphasis added). Saul thought little of himself even though God thought enough of him to make him king. He didn't have confidence in God. Fear was his fatal flaw. *Saul was afraid to fight Goliath* (1 Samuel 17). David had to slay the giant. Saul *feared David's popularity* with the people and tried to kill him several times. After Samuel had died, Saul feared yet another battle with the Philistines. God forbade the uses of mediums (see Leviticus 19:31, 20:6, and 20:27), but 1 Samuel 28 tells us that Saul was so afraid of the upcoming battle, he disguised himself and visited a medium. He asked her to call Samuel's spirit up from Sheol to ask him for advice. The results were disastrous. Samuel told Saul that God had torn the kingdom from him for this last act of disobedience and unfaithfulness. Samuel said the Philistines would kill him in battle the next day.

Samuel was right. The next day, the Philistines killed Saul's son Jonathan, and an arrow struck Saul between the links of his armor. He pleaded with his armor bearer to kill him *because he was afraid* of what the Philistines would do to him if they captured him alive. His armor bearer refused, so Saul fell on his own sword and died (see 1 Sam. 31:4-5). All these things happened to Saul because he clung to his fear rather than the God who had delivered him so many times in the past.

Elijah's response to fear was not as unfaithful as Gideon's, and Gideon's not as faithless as Saul's, but each had seen God do the miraculous in the past. God assured each that He was with them, and each focused on his fears rather than on God at moments of crisis. We may be disappointed by their response to fear, but if we're honest, we must admit that we're often like them. Even though we are believers, we still often embrace our fears rather than God. We're human. People with great faith will still be afraid sometimes. It's okay to be afraid. It's not okay to let fear paralyze us. We must overcome our fear. The accounts of these men are in the Bible to show us that we are not alone, and how to face our fears.

For many of us, our biggest fear is death. But God promised that, "...neither death, nor life, nor angels, nor principalities, nor things present, nor things to come, nor powers, nor height, nor depth, nor any other created thing, will be able to separate us from the love of God, which is in Christ Jesus our Lord" (Romans 8:38-39).

Most Christians would say that they aren't afraid of being dead. They fear the process of dying. That's completely natural.

But God says, "I will never leave you nor forsake you" (Heb. 13:5 ESV). We can only face down our fear if we trust that God is in control and that He loves us. If we keep our eyes on God and remember how He has delivered us in the past, we can have greater peace. Even death should not frighten us because we have God's promise that death can't separate us from Him, and that He will never forsake us.

What else do we fear? We fear men, failure, sickness, pain, job loss, poverty, rejection, and countless other things. God promises that He will supply everything we need. "Do not worry then, saying, 'What will we eat?' or 'What will we drink?' or 'What will we wear for clothing?' For the Gentiles eagerly seek all these things; for your heavenly Father knows that you need all these things. But seek first His kingdom and His righteousness, and all these things will be added to you" (Matt. 6:31-33).

God makes so many promises like this to us. When fear strikes, we need to take a deep breath, accurately evaluate the situation, remember God's past performance and provision, and trust Him.

## HOW SHOULD WE RESPOND TO FEAR?

These Biblical men strayed from the truth of what they knew about God. He is trustworthy and His promises are sure. They wilted under fear rather than persevering in God. So, how do we face fear head on?

### TRUST GOD'S PROMISES

Did you know that one of the Bible's most common commands is *fear not* or some variation of that phrase? It's used about 365 times in the Bible, once for each day of the year. Each time, God tells us to trust Him, to believe His promises, to allow God to be God, and to wait on His timing and goodness.

My favorite *fear not* verse is Isaiah 41:10: "Do not fear, for I am with you; Do not anxiously look about you, for I am your God. I will strengthen you, surely I will help you, Surely I will uphold you with My righteous right hand." If we trust God, our fears will diminish. When I'm flying and there is a lot of turbulence, I don't look at the other passengers or out the window. I look at the flight attendants. If they aren't nervous, then I'm not. It's all about where we look. Whatever we focus on becomes big and everything else becomes small. When we give space to our fear, fear becomes big and God becomes small. We can't allow God to become small in our thinking. We need to train ourselves to trust God and His promises. Then, He will loom large and our fears will diminish. Reverent fear, which is awe of God, keeps our eyes on Him.

### Remember that Jesus Is Powerful to Calm Our Fears

It may sound like *Christianese* or an empty platitude to say, "Trust God's promises," or "Re-direct your attention away from the things that cause fear and anxiety and on to God." But these are not empty words. Look what Jesus did when real-life people came to Him with their fears.

In Mark 4 and 5, there are several accounts of people coming to Jesus with their fear. For example, Jesus was in a boat crossing the Sea of Galilee with His apostles. He was asleep in the back of the boat when a great storm arose. His apostles woke Him and said to Him, "'Teacher, do You not care that we are perishing?' And He got up and rebuked the wind and said to the sea, 'Hush, be still.' And the wind died down and it became perfectly calm. And He said to them, 'Why are you afraid? Do you still have no faith?'" (Mark 4:38b-40).

His apostles feared the storm, the sea and death. Jesus showed He was sovereign over them all. This miracle is in the Bible to prove to us that Jesus can control nature. He is sovereign over everything we fear, even the storms, the sea, and death, because as believers, our eternity is secure.

In the next scene, after they crossed the sea, Jesus met a demon-possessed man whose name was Legion because so many demons possessed him. Jesus cast those demons into a large herd of swine which then ran down the hill and drowned in the sea. The herdsmen reported what Jesus had done in the town. Then the townspeople hurried to see what had happened. When they recognized the demoniac clothed and in his right mind, the townspeople became frightened and urged Jesus to leave. They didn't have reverent awe of Jesus. Instead, Jesus' power terrified them. But the man begged Jesus to allow him to come with Him. The demoniac experienced the miracle, and the crowd witnessed it (see Mark 5:1-20).

What was the difference between the demon-possessed man and the crowd? The man was in awe of Jesus and wanted to be with Him, but the crowd feared Him and wanted Him to go away. Jesus' power and grace changed the demon-possessed man, and it changes us too. One taste of His power to save, and His grace to be willing to save, and we want more and more.

In the very next scene in Mark, Jesus' raised Jairus' daughter and healed a woman who had been bleeding for twelve years. Jairus asked Jesus to come to his house to heal his daughter, who was sick and about to die. Time was of the essence; his daughter's life was ebbing away. Jesus was on his way when a crowd gathered around Him, impeding him. The bleeding woman inched forward, thinking, "This is my chance." She reached out in faith, believing that if she touched Jesus' garments, she would be made well. When she touched His robe, her bleeding stopped instantly.

Jesus knew someone had tapped into His power to heal and He demanded to know who touched Him. He knew who it was yet, Jesus asked to know who touched Him anyway, perhaps to see if the woman would come forward or to show His own disciples an example of true faith. The woman stepped forward and with fear (reverent awe), and trembling, confessed the whole truth. Jesus said, "Daughter, your faith has made you well; go in peace and be healed of your affliction" (see Mark 5:21-34).

While all this was going on, someone came and told Jairus not to bother Jesus anymore because his daughter had already died. Not exactly the most compassionate way to break unwelcome news, but thankfully Jesus was there. He said to Jairus, "Do not *be afraid* any longer, only believe." Jairus obediently led Jesus to his house where Jesus raised his daughter from the dead (See Mark 5:35-43).

The people in Mark 4 and 5 were all facing life and death situations. They were understandably afraid. They may not have had the strongest faith, but what faith they had was enough because Jesus was the object of their faith. Jesus said if you have faith the size of a mustard seed, you can move mountains (see Matt. 17:20). They each learned that Jesus is sovereign over all things, and He loved them enough to help. He moved the mountains in their lives. These stories show us that we can go to Jesus with our fears. Though He doesn't walk the earth now, He is just as alive and present as when He did. He is an ever-present help in time of trouble, and compassionate to help us face our fear.

.  .  .

### Change Your Lifestyle

Lifestyle changes can also help us re-direct our focus onto God. Here are some suggestions you might consider incorporating if you're not already doing so:

**a.** *Begin your day with prayer.* It's amazing how much fear God removes when we pray and read His promises in the Bible.

**b.** *Stay active.* Don't slump on the couch. Move. Get some exercise. I'm no doctor, but research shows that exercise decreases stress levels.

**c.** *Engage with other Christians.* Don't isolate yourself. People who have already experienced what you fear are an excellent source of comfort.

If you don't practice these suggestions regularly, try them. Prayer and lifestyle changes help.

## CONCLUSION

Now, back to the story of the dreaded trial. After two months of expecting to pick a jury and start the trial, the defendants finally increased their offer to the amount that my client had demanded. I guess it became too expensive for their clients to pay their thirty lawyers to come to court every day without resolving the case. I wasted so much time and energy in fear, and the trial never even happened. At the time, I wasn't even a believer. But I know now that God protected me from my biggest fear and still allowed my client to receive the funds needed to make repairs. I wasn't aware of it at the time, but God is sovereign over His creation and everything in it. If God protected us even when we were unbelievers, how much more can we rest in His goodness and love now that we're His children?

. . .

God has been faithful to lead me into a life in ministry, and I don't have to fear jury trials anymore. However, I'm not immune to other fears. I need to conquer them every day, just like anyone else. But I am learning to trust God's promises and remember His past faithfulness day by day, and that has helped me to manage my fear.

The second stanza of the great hymn by John Newton, "Amazing Grace," captures both senses of the word fear as I talked about above:

> 'Twas grace that taught
> My heart to fear (*reverent awe*)
> And grace my Fears (*terror*) relieved
> How precious did
> That grace appear
> The hour I first believed[2]

God loves us and wants us to trust Him. Revere Him and allow Him to take care of your fears.

# 3

# DOUBT

**"Are you the Expected One?" Luke 7:20**

I n October 2006, doctors diagnosed my good friend Brian with an aggressive form of leukemia. He lived in a hospital bed for two months and suffered greatly through chemotherapy and radiation. The cancer briefly moved into remission and he went home for Christmas. But right after Christmas the cancer returned. He spent the next four months in the hospital. During that time, I made the two-hour drive to the Hospital of the University of Pennsylvania to visit him twice. I wanted to have a spiritual conversation with him, to ask if he understood and believed the gospel, but he could barely communicate. On one visit, he managed to whisper a request that my church would pray for him. That gave me hope that he had faith.

Brian died on April 30, 2007. He was forty-two years old, and left behind a wife and four children ranging from six to twelve. Brian's death was the most tragic event I had experienced since coming to faith in 2004. I believed in God with all my heart, and had placed my faith in Jesus for my salvation, but my faith was new and untested. Again the nagging question returned. How could a good God allow such things? Is He unfair? Why wouldn't He stop this from happening? How could any good come from this? Brian's death shook my faith, and I began to doubt.

Several Bible characters had bouts with doubt. Abraham and Sarah doubted that they could have a child at their advanced age (Gen. 15, 17). Moses doubted he could lead the Israelites out of Egypt (Ex. 3:11). Gideon doubted that God could use him to rescue Israel from its enemies (Judges 6). All of those are fitting examples of God helping people despite their doubt. But I want to talk about a stunning example of doubt from the gospels: John the Baptist's.

## WHAT IS DOUBT?

Doubt means to be uncertain about something; to believe that something may not be true or is unlikely; or to have no confidence in something. Luke's gospel shows us how doubt invaded John the Baptist's life.

Luke wrote in Chapter 7,

"The disciples of John reported to him about all these things. Summoning two of his disciples, John sent them to the Lord, saying, 'Are You the Expected One, or do we look for someone else?' When the men came to Him, they said, "John the Baptist has sent us to You, to ask, 'Are You the Expected One, or do we look for someone else?'" At that very time He cured many *people* of diseases and afflictions and evil spirits; and He gave sight to many *who were* blind. And He answered and said to them, "Go and report to John what you have seen and heard: *the* blind receive sight, *the* lame walk, *the* lepers are cleansed, and *the* deaf hear, *the* dead are raised up, the poor have the gospel preached to them. Blessed is he who does not take offense at Me" (Luke 7:18-23).

Let's put this passage in its proper context. In Luke chapter 6, Jesus claimed that His words had authority. He said, "Why do you call me, 'Lord, Lord,' and do not do what I say?" He taught with authority and He expected the people to obey His teaching. In Luke 7:1-17, Jesus backed up His words with His works. He healed a centurion's slave without even being present, and raised a widow's son from the dead at a town called Nain. But while Jesus was doing all these things, John languished in a dark, cold, dingy prison on the east side of the Dead Sea, many miles from Jesus in Galilee. His crime, as we learn from Matthew 11, was rebuking Herod for taking his brother Philip's wife.

When John's disciples heard and told John about everything Jesus was doing, including his healing the centurion's slave and raising the widow's son, John sent two men to ask Jesus, "Are You the Expected One or should we expect someone else?" John's messengers traveled about seventy miles by foot in each direction to ask this question, so John clearly thought it very important. Why would he ask such a question?

## JOHN'S BACKGROUND

John's father, Zacharias, was one of about 18,000 Jewish priests serving in Jerusalem at that time. Priests were chosen by lot to burn incense in the temple just outside the Holy of Holies, the most sacred room in the temple. A priest would enter the temple to burn the incense twice daily for a week, an honor he could receive only once in his lifetime. Being chosen for this was the pinnacle of Zacharias's career. Zacharias's wife Elizabeth was barren, but the angel of the Lord met Zacharias and announced to him that God would give him and his wife Elizabeth a son.

The angel spoke to Zacharias of this child's future in Luke 1:17, "It is he who will go as a forerunner before Him [the Messiah] in the spirit and power of Elijah, to turn the hearts of the fathers back to the children, and the disobedient to the attitude of the righteous, so as to make ready a people prepared for the Lord." As a priest trained in the Scriptures, Zacharias would have known from Malachi 3 and Isaiah 40 that a forerunner would precede the Messiah. But Zacharias didn't believe that his barren wife could conceive. He said to the angel Gabriel in Luke 1:18: "How will I know this *for certain*? For I am an old man and my wife is advanced in years." He had to suffer the consequences of his doubt. The angel of the Lord closed his mouth, so he could not speak until after John's birth.

After John's birth, and after Zacharias named him John as the angel had commanded, God restored his ability to speak. Zacharias then prophesied about his son, "For you will go before the Lord to prepare His ways, to give his people knowledge of their salvation through the forgiveness of sins." Zacharias would have taught these things to John throughout his childhood. Think about Prince Charles of England. He has known from the time he was a little boy that someday he will be King of England. In the same way, John understood that one day he would serve as the forerunner for the Messiah.

When John was old enough, he went into the desert and began preaching a baptism of repentance for the forgiveness of sin. Jesus met him there in the wilderness and John baptized him. At that moment, John saw the Holy Spirit descend on Jesus like a dove, and he heard these words: "This is my Son and in Him I am well pleased." John witnessed all of this before Herod shackled him in prison. While he was in prison, he heard about the miraculous things that Jesus did. But as time went on, doubt crept in.

Why? John expected Jesus to do more than miraculous healings. He understood that Israel's Messiah would give sight to the blind (Isaiah 61:1, 29:18, 35:5, 42:18) make the lame to walk (Isaiah 35:6), cleanse lepers, cure deafness (Isaiah 19:18, 35:5, 42:18), raise the dead (Isaiah 26:19), preach good news to the poor, and "free the captives" (Isaiah 61:1). This would ring very relevant to John wasting away in jail. Jews also expected the Messiah to restore the nation of Israel to the glory it enjoyed under David. First century Jews expected a military messiah who would deliver them from the Romans. That's what the promise to "free the captives" meant to them, and to John. John probably expected that Jesus would rescue him and that he would help Jesus overthrow Rome. Yet, Jesus did not appear to be mobilizing an army.

Have you ever seen, *The Shawshank Redemption*? It's one of my favorite movies. In one scene, the warden punished Andy Dufresne, the hero, with sixty days of solitary confinement for calling him obtuse. Can you imagine sixty days of dark, cold isolation? John faced the same cold, dark isolation. So, when John asked Jesus if He was the expected one, he was asking if Jesus was the awaited Messiah. If so, where was the kingdom of God? Why was Rome still in power? And why was John in prison?

## THE REASON FOR DOUBT

John doubted for the same reason that you and I do: unfulfilled expectations. They always produce dissatisfaction and disappointment. On a recent flight from Los Angeles to Dallas, the pilot announced that we caught a strong tailwind and would land thirty minutes early. Everyone cheered. When we landed, he returned with the unwelcome news that because we landed so early, there was no gate open for us. We would wait on the tarmac for thirty minutes before he could park the plane. Everyone booed!

Even though we exited the plane precisely as scheduled, the pilot had changed our expectations. People in the service industry know that when you tell people how long they'll have to wait, you estimate on the high side. They'll be happy when their wait is shorter than they expected. It's all about creating proper expectations. The phrase, "under-promise, over-deliver" comes to mind. When we get less than we expect, we will always be disappointed.

When we harbor unrealistic expectations about God, disappointment follows, and that disappointment can lead to doubt. In the story I told about Brian at the beginning of the chapter, wrong expectations about God caused me not only to be disappointed with God, but to doubt Him too. God's ideas about how long Brian should live, and about what is fair are different than mine. Not fully understanding God's plan caused me to doubt Him. God was not the problem. I was.

As reasonable beings, we sometimes think we should be able to understand everything that God does. We give ourselves far too much credit. The gap between God's intelligence and ours is immeasurable. God doesn't explain Himself to us, and we shouldn't expect that of Him. God never told Job why He allowed him to suffer. After God thundered at Job, Job didn't ask any more questions. Instead, he repented and acknowledged God's sovereignty. God owes us no explanation for what He does and why He does it. We wouldn't understand His explanation anyway. God's thoughts are above ours. Explaining them to us is like us trying to teach algebra to a dog.

John expected Jesus to rescue Israel from the Romans. He did not understand that God planned for the coming of the Messiah to be a two-part act. Jesus came the first time not to save the Jews from the Romans, but to save people from their sin. He will come again a second time to conquer His enemies and establish His kingdom. Some things happen now, and some things later. How could John have understood that? Like us, John wanted everything now. We moan and groan when we experience trying circumstances. It's difficult, if not impossible to see God working during our suffering. John could not fathom how God's plan could include him suffering through an unjust prison sentence. Wrong expectations caused disappointment and then doubt.

## THE THINGS WE DOUBT

Now before we condemn John for his doubt, realize that we place wrong expectations on God every day. We wonder why we suffer, or why things don't turn out for us as we think they should. When loved ones die or we have a financial downturn, or when we're diagnosed with cancer, we think He has failed us or abandoned us. Why does God allow these things? As finite creatures, we experience events sequentially in time. We measure our suffering in minutes, hours, days, and sometimes years. But God is not bound by time. God sees all of eternity all at once. He knows the beginning and the end and everything in the middle. His ways are higher than our ways and His thoughts are higher than our thoughts (Is. 55:8-9). Our discomfort that seems so long and hard to us, is merely a blip compared to eternity.

John was experiencing the same thing. He did not understand why he was suffering in prison, so he asked Jesus a very human question. It's the same question I would have asked: "Are you the Expected One or should we look for another?"

When we doubt, what is it that we are uncertain about? Do we doubt that God is good? Or that God cares? Do we doubt that God hears our prayers? Are we questioning whether God has the power to change our circumstances? Do we wonder if God would stoop to intervene in our lives when each of us is just one of 7.5 billion people on this planet? These questions are the normal human response to what we perceive as God's inactivity in our lives.

I propose that we ask better questions. The questions to ask are not the *why* questions. Why is God allowing this? Why won't God intervene? Why doesn't God care? We should be asking *what* and *how* questions. What does God want me to learn in my circumstances? How can I be a blessing to others through my experience? How can I become more like Christ through this trial? If we ask better questions, we will get better answers. We can turn our unhealthy doubt into greater understanding that God uses suffering to work in our lives.

## IS IT WRONG TO DOUBT?

Jesus never rebuked John for his doubt. Rather, He reassured John's messengers by showing them that His actions matched the prophecies about Israel's Messiah. "**At that very time**, He [Jesus] cured many people of diseases and afflictions and evil spirits; and He gave sight to many who were blind. (Luke 7:21-22 emphasis added). Jesus allowed John's messengers to be eyewitnesses of his miracles before He answered. How often has God allowed us to be eyewitnesses to His work? Has God used you to bring friends or family members to saving faith? Have you seen your sick friends or family healed? Have you watched God work out the impossible in your life? Those are miracles that God has allowed you to observe to help you when doubt creeps in. **Remind yourself of God's blessings when you begin to doubt.**

After performing miracles that showed He was the Messiah, Jesus told John's messengers to go and report to him, "The blind receive sight, the lame walk, those who have leprosy are cleansed, the deaf hear, the dead are raised and the good news is proclaimed to the poor" (Luke 7:22). Jesus reassured John that He was the promised One, by doing exactly what the OT prophecy, especially Isaiah 35 and 61, predicted He would do.

Jesus concluded His speech to John's messengers by sending John encouragement that, "Blessed is he who does not take offense at Me" (Luke 7:23). Jesus understood John's doubt. He wanted to reassure John that he had properly placed his faith in Him. Faith is a complex thing and doubts easily arise. When they do, we want reassurance too. What prison do you currently occupy? Obviously, I'm not talking about a physical prison. Are you imprisoned by health issues, financial troubles, conflict with your kids or spouse, job insecurity, problems with addiction, fear of what is happening in the world today? You may see no way out of these problems. Like John, doubts arise.

. . .

OSWALD CHAMBERS, AUTHOR OF *MY UTMOST FOR HIS HIGHEST* wrote, "Doubt is not always a sign that a man is wrong, it may be a sign that he is thinking."[1] Doubt is not wrong if it causes us to ask healthy questions of God. Doubt does not equal denial. Even great giants of faith like Moses, David, Elijah and Jeremiah had doubts. Look what Jesus says to the crowd after John's messengers leave:

> When the messengers of John had left, He began to speak to the crowds about John, "What did you go out into the wilderness to see? A reed shaken by the wind? But what did you go out to see? A man dressed in soft clothing? Those who are splendidly clothed and live in luxury are found in royal palaces! But what did you go out to see? A prophet? Yes, I say to you, and one who is more than a prophet. This is the one about whom it is written, 'Behold, I send My messenger ahead of You, Who will prepare Your way before You.' I say to you, among those born of women there is no one greater than John; yet he who is least in the kingdom of God is greater than he." When all the people and the tax collectors heard this, they acknowledged God's justice, having been baptized with the baptism of John. But the Pharisees and the lawyers rejected God's purpose for themselves, not having been baptized by John (Luke 7:24-30).

After John's messengers left to take Jesus' message back to him, Jesus delivered a second speech, this time to the crowd. He praised John as a prophet, and even more than a prophet, despite his doubts. Jesus' reference to "a reed shaken by the wind" symbolizes a compromiser who sways to the most recent popular opinion. John was not that. A man dressed in fancy clothes lives in palaces. John lived in the wilderness, not in palaces. John had integrity and the strength of his convictions.

He landed in prison for challenging King Herod and scolding him because he violated Moses' law by marrying his brother's wife. No one could call John a wimp. The people traveled out to the desert to see a prophet. Jesus affirmed that John was a prophet, but more than just *a* prophet. He fulfilled the prophecy about *the prophet* predicted in the scriptures who would prepare the way for the Messiah [see Isaiah 40, Malachi 3]. Jesus also said, "…among those born of women there is no one greater than John" (Luke 7:28). That would make John the greatest human who had lived to that point. That's high praise for one who had great doubt.

Jesus went on to proclaim in the second half of verse 28, "Yet, the one who is least in the kingdom of God is greater than he." This statement showed the greatness of the kingdom of heaven. The least member in the kingdom of heaven exceeds the glory of the greatest prophet on earth. God welcomed John into heaven despite his doubt. His doubt did not alter his destination.

## DOUBT VS. UNBELIEF

We might wonder, if John was such a great prophet, then why did he remain in prison? We learn the answer in verses 29 and 30. The crowd consisted of two distinct groups: First, there were common, uneducated people who had believed John's message and now followed Jesus. "All the people, even the tax collectors, when they heard Jesus' words, acknowledged that God's way was right, because they had been baptized by John" (v. 29).

The second group present were the educated and elitist Pharisees and scribes. They responded differently. "But the Pharisees and the experts in the law *rejected God's purpose for themselves*, because they had not been baptized by John" (v. 30, emphasis added). The powerful and influential rejected John. By refusing to repent and receive John's baptism, they not only rejected John, they rejected God's will for their lives. Thus, they also rejected Jesus. These were the leaders of Jewish society. They knew their Scriptures, but chose denial and willful unbelief. Henry Drummond, an author and evangelist from the 1800's, wrote, "Christ never failed to distinguish between doubt and unbelief. Doubt is can't believe. Unbelief is won't believe. Doubt is honesty. Unbelief is obstinacy. Doubt is looking for light. Unbelief is content with darkness."[2]

When the New Testament refers to people who doubt, it is usually talking about believers. Abraham, Moses, David, Elijah, and many others believed but had periods of doubt. Let's be honest. We all waver from time to time. The harder our circumstances, the more we tend to doubt. In a sermon entitled, "Solving the Problem of Doubt," John MacArthur said, "You have to believe something first before you can doubt it. You have to be committed to it before you question it." [3]

So the answer to our question is that it is not wrong to have doubt if our doubt leads us to fall on our knees in prayer to seek answers from God. Doubt does not equal denial. This leads to a final question.

## WHAT IS THE ANTIDOTE TO DOUBT?

Allow me to offer a few suggestions. If we remain disciplined about what to do when we inevitably face doubt, our faith will ultimately be strengthened rather than weakened. Put these habits into practice.

. . .

### Don't allow doubt to turn into denial

Compare John and the Pharisees. John didn't understand, so he earnestly and genuinely sought answers to his doubt. David did the same thing throughout the Psalms, and he was a man after God's own heart. Jesus praised John, but He rejected the Pharisees. The fact that John doubted should be encouraging to us. Sometimes we might think that if we walked and talked with Jesus, like John did, we would never doubt. But even John wrestled with doubt. We must also remember that John didn't know what we know. He did not live to see Jesus' resurrection or the Holy Spirit's arrival at Pentecost. We have the advantage of living on this side of the cross. We have the New Testament. We know Jesus' identity better than John did, even though we are living 2000 years later. We have no excuse for letting doubt turn into denial. Go to Jesus with your doubt!

### Resolve not to allow our circumstances to harden our hearts

John was in prison and confused. When we experience doubt, we must remember that God wants us to become like Christ, even at the expense of our comfort. God uses our struggles to make us more like His Son. When we endure trials by responding in faith, we prove our faith and strengthen it. When we look for God's purposes in what He allows to come our way, we learn to see how God uses our circumstances to bring glory to Himself. Keep your eyes on Jesus during difficult times when faith is weak, so doubt doesn't harden your heart.

### When doubts rise up in our minds, let's fall on our knees

Resolve that when you doubt you will seek Jesus more, not less. Press in. Seek understanding, wisdom, and how God may be working in your life. Try to look at your circumstances from God's perspective and discern what He wants to accomplish through them. Jesus will never reject someone who wants to understand Him better. Jesus only rejects the one who rejects Him. I believe that the purpose of this passage is to show us that God can handle our doubts. When you doubt, ask healthy questions. Like John, we need to seek understanding. Let's be like the man in Mark 9:24, who said to Jesus, "Lord, I believe. Help my unbelief."

## CONCLUSION

Brian's death tested my faith. At some point in my grieving process, I said to God, "Lord, I am never going to understand some things about You or some of the things that You allow. But I trust You based on Your character, and Jesus' work on the cross, no matter what." When I was struggling the most with doubt, God pointed me back to the cross. Always remember the cross. *It is there that God proved His love for us.* I still doubt occasionally, but I find reassurance in the cross *and the resurrection.*

When doubts afflict you, don't let them turn into denial. Don't harden your heart against God because of difficult circumstances. *When doubts rise in your minds, fall on your knees in prayer.* Seek wisdom and understanding. God will TRANSFORM your doubt into strengthened faith. Here's how hymn-writer Albert Simpson said it:

> O doubting, struggling Christian,
> Why thus in anguish pray?
> O cease to doubt and struggle,
> There is a better way.

O settle it all with Jesus,
O settle it all today;

O cease to doubt and struggle,
O cease to plead and pray;
O rest in His word forever,
And settle it all today.[4]

# 4

# REJECTION

**"Isn't this the Carpenter?" Mark 6:3**

When I was in the fifth grade, one of the boys in my class hosted a tenth birthday party. He invited every boy in our class except me. I thought that we were friends, but I guess I was wrong. I'll never forget how much that feeling of rejection hurt. Still today, forty-five years later I remember it like it happened yesterday. It broke my ten-year-old heart. I wondered, "What did I do to deserve that?" How had I offended my supposed friend? I don't know. I never asked. Maybe I was afraid to confront him. Maybe I didn't want to know the answer. That incident has stuck with me my entire life.

I had thirteen ushers in my wedding party because I loved them all and didn't want any of them to feel rejected. Why draw lines? I shared this story with my kids many times while they were planning parties and playdates to emphasize to them that we never, ever, ever, leave anyone out of the fun. We made our daughter and son invite children to their parties and playdates that they didn't even like, but I didn't care. To me, better to cast a wide net to save some kid the agony of rejection so painful that he needed to write about it forty-five years later!

Rejection is painful, embarrassing, and shameful. We always want to be part of the group. We never want to feel left out. Unfortunately, rejection is a part of life. When you tried out for a sports team, you exposed your skills, or lack thereof, to the coach who had the power to make cuts. When you asked the girl that you had liked since freshman year to the prom, you knew that you were putting your heart in her hands. When your friends rented an apartment together without you, that really hurt. When you applied to college, you knew some anonymous admissions officer held your fate in his or her hands. When you worked for a company for forty years, and your boss said it was time for you to retire, you felt marginalized. Anytime you applied for a job, asked the bank for a loan, tried to share the gospel, or a million other ways that you put yourself out on a limb, you risked rejection.

We have all put our hearts, talents, qualifications, or beliefs in someone else's hands, knowing that we have left ourselves completely vulnerable to the whims of that person's decision. We said in effect, "Here I am. Do with me what you will." We hope for acceptance, but rejection is always a possibility.

If you're a believer in Jesus Christ, rejection is almost a certainty. But we should not be surprised by that, because Jesus endured rejection too.

When Jesus walked the earth, He lived the first thirty years of His life in relative obscurity. He lived a quiet life at home, obeyed His parents, and learned His father's trade. It wasn't until He began His public ministry and stepped out from the crowd that He truly risked rejection. In other words, it wasn't until He answered the call placed on His life that He experienced the rejection of the world.

Jesus left home, became an itinerant preacher, claimed to be the Son of God, commanded people to repent of their sins, challenged traditional beliefs, and confronted the ruling authorities. Rejection was one thing coming from the rulers and the religious leaders. Those were the very people He was challenging and confronting, so it was to be expected. But as we will see, the most painful rejections came from those closest to Him, His own friends and family in his hometown.

## CAUSES OF REJECTION

There are many reasons why people will reject us. Let's look at some of the reasons why people rejected Jesus and see if we recognize them in our own circumstances.

### JEALOUSY

In Mark 5, Jesus miraculously healed the twelve-year-old daughter of a synagogue leader named Jairus. He also cured a woman who had been bleeding for twelve years, after she spent all that she had on doctors only to have her condition worsen. He fearlessly freed a man from demon possession and restored him to his right mind. After performing these miracles, Jesus returned to His hometown of Nazareth. Let's pick up the story in Mark 6. Verse 1 says, "Jesus left there and went to His hometown accompanied by His disciples." I try to imagine myself as one of the disciples returning home to Nazareth. I would be expecting a ticker-tape parade after all the miracles that Jesus had done. "Hey Peter, can you imagine what all our friends are going to say when they see us returning with the

Master? We're gonna be rock stars!" They were about to be disappointed.

On the Sabbath, Jesus began to teach in the synagogue and the people were amazed. They seemed amazed in a positive way, as if impressed with Him, and as though they would receive His teaching with joy. But that's not how it was.

> "Where did this man get these things," they asked. "What's this wisdom that has been given Him? What are these remarkable miracles he is performing? Isn't this the carpenter? Isn't this Mary's son and the brother of James, Joseph, Judas and Simon? Aren't his sisters here with us? And they took offense at him" (Mark 6:2-3 NIV).

His own people rejected Him. Isn't that something? Perhaps some context will shed light on this event. Nazareth was a small village to the west of the Sea of Galilee. It was near other small villages, and word of what Jesus was doing would have traveled fast. The people in Nazareth had heard about the miracles that He had been performing. They listened to His teaching. Yet they rejected Him anyway. Why? Most likely it's because they knew Him. They knew His family. They thought He was elevating Himself above them by the things He was doing, and they weren't going to stand for that.

They asked mocking questions. "Isn't he the carpenter," was meant to demean Him. They tried to disgrace Him by calling Him Mary's son rather than Joseph's son. Joseph had probably died by this time, but even if a son's father had died and left his mother a widow, people would still identify him as his father's son.[1] They were intentionally affronting Him by suggesting that His mother conceived Him under questionable circumstances. Jesus did not miss the nuances of their insults. He lamented in verse 4, "A prophet is not without honor except in his hometown and among his own relatives and among his own household." Verse six says He was amazed at their unbelief and then went out from them to other cities.

The Jewish rulers were undoubtedly jealous of Jesus. Jesus predicted several times that He must "suffer many things and be rejected by the leaders and the chief priests and the scribes, and be killed, and after three days rise again" (see Mark 8:31; Luke 17:25). When the Jewish leaders arrested Jesus and handed Him over to Pilate, Mark's gospel tells us that Pilate, "was aware that the chief priests had handed Him over because of envy" (Mark 15:10). They were envious because people were leaving them to follow Jesus. He was disrupting the status quo and needed to be stopped. They could not argue against His wisdom and His teaching on the purpose of the Sabbath or with the many parables He spoke against them. He turned every trap that they laid for Him back on themselves. The people watched Jesus humiliate the leaders and chief priests repeatedly. That's why they wanted Him dead. Jealousy blinded them. They did not see that Jesus was indeed the Messiah that He claimed to be, and they crucified Him.

Jealousy was not new in Jesus' day. It had been around since Cain killed Abel. Indeed, jealousy is and has been rampant throughout the lineage of God's chosen people. You'll recall that Joseph was Jacob's favorite son, the son of his beloved wife, Rachel. Joseph's brothers despised his position as their father's favorite. They hated that Jacob made him a multi-colored coat and made nothing for them. Jacob went out of his way to show that Joseph was his favorite. His brothers' jealousy burned against Joseph when he told them about his dream of their ears of corn bowing down to his. It wasn't wise of him to report his dreams to his brothers, but as a seventeen-year-old young man,

Joseph lacked prudence. He didn't perceive that their jealousy could have such disastrous results. Their jealousy led them to sell him as a slave to a caravan of passing Midianites headed for Egypt.

Moses also faced the jealousy of his siblings. God anointed Moses to lead Israel out of Egypt and into the promised land. Yet, in true human fashion, his own sister, Miriam, and brother, Aaron, spoke against him. They said, "Has the Lord indeed spoken only through Moses? Has He not spoken through us as well? And the Lord heard it" (Num. 12:2). They were jealous of their brother. They wanted their own share of glory. The Lord punished Miriam by making her leprous. God did not restore her until Moses prayed for her. Even so, the Lord left her leprous and outside the camp for seven days before He healed her. A common thread in these biblical stories is that human jealousy is a catalyst for rejection.

### FEAR

Another reason that we will face rejection is because of fear. People will calculate what belief will cost them. They will count the cost of befriending us too. If association with us threatens their comfort, they will reject us. Jesus experienced this from His own family.

We've already noted how the people in Jesus' hometown rejected Him because of jealousy. But this wasn't the first time Jesus' family had scorned Him. In Mark 3, Jesus entered a house, and again a crowd gathered, so that he and his disciples couldn't even eat. "When his family heard about this, they went to take charge of him, for they said, 'He is out of his mind'" (Mark 3:21 NIV). Jesus had healed many people of illness, driven demons out of people, and had regularly taught in the synagogues around Galilee. Why would His own family say that He was out of His mind? I believe the reason was fear. They were afraid that He was becoming a fanatic who would attract the attention of the religious authorities and bring disgrace upon the family. They wanted Him to come home, leave the public spotlight, allow the recognition that He was receiving to subside, and return to normal life. They didn't want the kind of notoriety that He was bringing. If they were associated with a religious fanatic, the religious officials could expel them from the synagogue, which was the equivalent of being a social outcast. The social consequences of aligning themselves with Jesus were severe.

If you want a testament to the power of fear, consider Jesus' mother. Mary had received the message from the angel Gabriel that the Holy Spirit would conceive a child within her. He told her that this child would be the Messiah of Israel, and she was still afraid to follow her Son (Mark 3:31-35). Fear can blind us to truth. Mary knew that Jesus was God's Son, and yet she still feared what people might think about her or do to her if she pledged allegiance to Him. She may have been following the lead of her older sons since Joseph was probably dead by this time, and it's also possible that she came to support Jesus.

On the other hand, Mary seemed to be quite assertive when she wanted to be. She was quite vocal in John chapter 2 when she wanted Jesus to turn the water into wine. It's impossible to know whether Mary, or her older sons was leading this charge. However, the point remains. Neither Mary, or Jesus' brothers were willing to suffer embarrassment or potential economic setbacks for Jesus. Fear can lead to rejection.

\* \* \*

## MISUNDERSTANDING

Misunderstanding happens when you expect someone to deliver something they never intended to deliver. Judas expected Jesus to usher in a physical kingdom on earth. Jesus did not intend to do that.

Of course, Jesus' eleven other apostles didn't understand Him either. When the soldiers arrested Jesus in the garden on the night Judas betrayed Him, His friends all abandoned Him. As Jesus predicted, Peter denied Him three times. That kind of rejection is painful enough. But Judas betrayed Him—with a kiss! Judas' actions put the trial and crucifixion of Jesus into motion. I believe it was because Judas misunderstood Jesus' mission. I believe that Judas expected Israel's Messiah to restore Israel to its former glory under David and Solomon 1000 years earlier. Jesus was not the military Messiah that Judas expected from his reading of the Hebrew Scriptures. Jesus spoke of loving your enemies, turning the other cheek, walking two miles when your enemy makes you walk one. Jesus said, "Blessed are the meek for they will inherit the earth." I think these sounded like wimpy words to Judas. And yet Jesus claimed to be the Messiah.

Judas was confused, impatient, and eager for change. Sick and tired of waiting for Jesus to fight, Judas tried to force Jesus' hand. "If He's arrested and facing death," Judas thought, "He'll have no choice other than to move against His enemies and usher in the kingdom." We can't know for sure what Judas' motives were, but many experts believe Judas betrayed Jesus because Jesus didn't mobilize forces against Rome. The thirty pieces of silver paid to Judas by the Jewish leaders was further incentive.

Judas misunderstood Jesus' mission. Jesus did intend to reign over a kingdom on earth, but not yet. Like John the

Baptist, Judas couldn't understand that Jesus' mission would be in two separate comings. The first time He came was to live a perfect, sinless life, which qualified Him to pay the sin debt that we owe. Then He died on a cross to make payment for our sins, so God would not have to punish us for our sins if we believe in Him. He came to show us the way to salvation.

The second time Jesus comes, He will judge and rule His enemies. Believers will receive heaven and eternal rewards. Jesus will cast unbelievers into outer darkness. Judas misunderstood Jesus' mission. I think Judas tried to force Jesus to topple Rome, something He never intended to do. When Jesus didn't, Judas rejected Him, and betrayed Him to the Jewish authorities.

Jealousy, fear, and misunderstanding cause a significant amount of rejection. We've all suffered rejection for one, if not all, of those reasons. But there are other reasons for rejection. Colleges deny admission because of poor test scores and grades. Employers hire someone else if we don't have enough experience or the proper skill set. Banks deny our loan because our poor credit shows that we are a financial risk. Rejection hurts!

Most of us have suffered rejection because of our faith in Jesus as well. If you're a new believer but didn't grow up in a Christian church, your family may have a challenging time understanding your new-found faith. They may reject you as Jesus' family rejected Him. Even if our family accepts us for our faith, much of society will not. People will call us arrogant, foolish, stupid and many other names because we insist that Jesus is the *only* way to heaven. They will think that Jesus' exclusivity claim is narrow-minded and intolerant. This is the world we live in now. It ignores or misunderstands that even though Christianity is exclusive in its beliefs—you must believe the gospel to be a Christian—it is inclusive because Jesus invites *everyone* to come and to believe the good news of the gospel of Jesus Christ. But rather than accept the invitation, most will spurn the message and the Messenger.

Jesus expected this. He said:

> "If the world hates you, you know that it has hated Me before it hated you. If you were of the world, the world would love its own; but because you are not of the world, but I chose you out of the world, because of this the world hates you. Remember the word that I said to you, 'A slave is not greater than his master.' If they persecuted Me, they will also persecute you; if they kept My word, they will keep yours also (John 15:18-20).

Later in John's gospel, Jesus told them: "In this world you will have trouble, but take heart, I have overcome the world!" Then Jesus prayed for them because they would remain in the world.

> I have given them Your word; and the world has hated them, because they are not of the world, even as I am not of the world. I do not ask You to take them out of the world, but to keep them from the evil one. They are not of the world, even as I am not of the world. Sanctify them in the truth; Your word is truth. As You sent Me into the world, I also have sent them into the world (John 17:14-18).

Jesus sent His apostles into the world, knowing that the world would reject them. He prayed for them to have the strength to withstand that rejection and continue to witness for Him in the world. He knew that enemies would make trouble for them, but He also knew that their mission would be successful. That's why He prayed for those who would believe through the apostles' testimony. That includes you and me. Read Jesus' prayer:

> I do not ask on behalf of these alone, but for those also who believe in Me through their word; that they may all be one; even as You, Father, are in Me and I in You, that they also may be in Us, so that the world may believe that You sent Me (John 17:20-21).

It should come as no surprise that we will face rejection. That may not make it any easier to deal with, but the fact that Jesus prayed for us 2000 years ago to be able to stand up against the rejection of the world should give us comfort and strength. If Jesus prayed it, we can trust that His prayer was effective, and that we will be able to bear the world's rejection of us.

## RESPONSES TO REJECTION

So how should we respond when we face the world's rejection? Rejection is part of the human experience. It's part of what Jesus suffered, and part of what the author of Hebrews referenced when he wrote that "Jesus is not a high priest who is unable to sympathize with our weakness" (Heb. 4:15). Jesus experienced every rejection that we have and more. He even experienced God the Father's rejection on the cross. As Jesus bled and suffocated to death He said, "My God, my God, why have you forsaken me?" (Matthew 27:46). It was the only time Jesus ever experienced that anguish of separation from God in all of eternity. He faced separation from His Father because of His passion to take our sin on Himself, so we who believe in Him would be declared righteous. So here are some things we can do when rejection smacks us in the face.

### PLAY TO AN AUDIENCE OF ONE

If it is our goal in life to obtain the approval of people, we will experience disappointment often. People pleasers can never truly please anyone long term. The people we aim to satisfy will either raise their standard or change their minds. When we fail in their eyes, they will reject us. That's why it's foolish to try to please people, and why we should not find our identity on the approval of others. People are fickle and unpredictable at best. At worst, they can be legalistic, mean, or even oppressive.

God is not like people. (How's that for an understatement?!) The writer of Hebrews tells us, "Jesus is the same yesterday, today and forever" (Heb. 13:8). That means we can know how to please God because His standard never changes. He wants us to believe in His Son and repent of our sin. The reward is eternal life. But God also wants us to live a holy life. We will never be sinless, but we can sin less. We should strive every day to live a life that pleases God, even if people reject us for it. The Lord said on the night He was betrayed, "He who has My commandments and keeps them is the one who loves me" (John 14:21). When we begin to live a holy life, our friends will either be drawn to us because of Christ, or they will reject us and drift away. They won't want to feel like we are judging them. It's OK. While we grieve for our lost friends, we'll make new friends who will accept us as we are, and as we will be, as God continues to work in our lives. Most importantly, we'll please God. Live a life pleasing to the only One who matters, and don't worry about rejection by the world.

. . .

### KNOW THE TRUTH

One of the worst things about rejection is that it causes us to feel shame, damages our self-image, and can cause us to lapse into self-pity. That's a dangerous cycle that can spiral down into anxiety, depression, and other more serious disorders. We must look at ourselves the way that God looks at us even when the world rejects us. "For God so loved the world that He gave His only Son that whoever believes in Him shall not perish but have eternal life" (John 3:16). You may have that verse memorized. But have you ever really meditated on it? Why would God send His Son? Why would Jesus die on a cross for you and for me? Because He thought we were worth it.

No matter how we may be feeling about ourselves in the face of rejection, God esteems us so highly and loves us so much, that He sent His one and only Son to die for us. Jesus paid an infinite price to redeem you and me. Now considering that truth, we insult Him when we let the world cause us to have low self-esteem, and when we wallow in self-pity. God doesn't see us that way, so why should we see ourselves that way? If the God of the universe thought that we were worth dying for, why should we care if some person rejects us?

### DEVELOP A THICK SKIN

Jesus said, "The one who listens to you listens to me and the one who rejects you rejects me" (Luke 10:16). Just as a quarterback shouldn't take too much recognition when the team wins or too much blame when the team loses, so we shouldn't take credit if people receive our message or feel shame if they reject it. We don't rejoice in ourselves or accept praise when they listen to us, because they are receiving Jesus by the power of the Holy Spirit.

I like when people pay attention or tell me they learned something when I preach, or that my message was just what they needed to hear that day. I spend a lot of time preparing, but truthfully, they're not really listening to me, they're listening to the word of God. Without the Bible, I have nothing to say. With the Bible, I have tons to say! It seems like I am the one taking a risk when I speak a message from God, or if I write a book like this one. But really, I'm just the messenger. If they reject me, they are rejecting the One who sent the message.

In 1 Samuel 8, the people demanded that Samuel appoint a king over Israel like the other nations had. Their plea grieved Samuel and he asked the Lord for counsel. The Lord said to Samuel, "Listen to the voice of the people in regard to all that they say to you, for they have not rejected you, but they have rejected Me from being king over them" (1 Sam 8:7). Samuel was just the messenger. They did not reject Samuel; they rejected God.

When two countries are at war, the leader of one country may send an ambassador with an offer of terms of peace. If the leader of the other country refuses, he has rejected the one who sent the ambassador. The ambassador only relays the message of rejection. The bottom line is that as ambassadors for Jesus, we need to develop thick skin. People will reject us sometimes.

## CONCLUSION

If we know that rejection is inevitable for a believer, how can we prepare ourselves for it so it doesn't shock us when it happens?

**1. Expect Rejection.** We should expect it because Jesus told us it would happen. Life experience teaches us that we can't avoid it. We all face rejection in one way or another almost every single day. Knowing that it's part of the Christian's daily life can prepare us for it.

**2. Don't Accept Rejection.** Even though we should expect rejection, we don't have to accept it. David wrote in Psalm 27: "Do not hide Your face from me, Do not turn Your servant away in anger; You have been my help; Do not abandon me nor forsake me, O God of my salvation! For my father and my mother have forsaken me, But the Lord will take me up" (Psalm 27:9-10). Isn't that amazing? We don't know the event that David was referring to in this psalm, but his own father and mother rejected Him. Even so, he had confidence that the Lord would take him up. Never let the rejection of others put a speed bump in your road. Your own family may reject you, but God never will.

\* \* \*

A FOOTNOTE TO THE STORY OF NOT BEING INVITED TO THAT birthday party forty-five years ago. About a year later, my family moved from that town to a new town just two miles away. I told my friends that I would stay in touch with them. It should have been easy. It was just a short bike ride. But as soon as we got to our new town, I made new friends. I didn't forget my old friends, but I made no effort to see them and they made no effort to see me. I'm not blaming them. It was my fault as much as theirs. We were young, and life goes on. My point is that we waste so much time and effort seeking the approval of others so desperately, and often the people whose approval we want the most will not be part of our lives in one year, five years, or ten years.

Read the beautiful words of "Hail Thou Once Despised Jesus," by hymn-writer John Bakewell.

Hail, thou once despised Jesus!
Hail, thou Galilean King!
Thou didst suffer to release us,
thou didst free salvation bring.

Hail, thou agonizing Savior,
bearer of our sin and shame!
By thy merits we find favor,
life is given thro' thy name.[2]

Rejection by others is unimportant compared to God's approval, and fleeting compared to God's eternal love and acceptance. Put the approval of others in its proper perspective.

# 5

# TEMPTATION

**"You will be like God" Genesis 3:5**

I have always been fascinated with astronomy. I love to gaze up at the stars on a clear night. I even have an app on my phone that identifies the constellations, stars, and planets when I point my phone up into the sky. When I entered college, I hadn't decided on a major, but I knew I wanted to take a couple of astronomy classes. As it turns out, astronomy is a whole lot more calculus and physics than it is staring up at the night sky. I didn't take either of those classes in high school, so I was in way over my head in a big hurry. My interest in astronomy gave way to a new interest, surviving the class.

When the midterm exam came around, I knew I was not likely to pass. I hadn't learned the material or sought help from the professor. My class attendance was spotty at best. I deserved to fail, but I didn't want to fail. By now, you have probably figured out how this story ends. The mid-term exam was a multiple-choice test, and temptation to glance at my neighboring classmates' desks overcame me. In other words, I cheated. I'm not proud of it. I'm not trying to excuse it. But I didn't think I had another viable choice if I wanted to pass the test. My failure to prepare left me vulnerable to the temptation to cheat, and I succumbed.

## WHAT IS TEMPTATION?

When I speak of temptation, I'm describing it the way the Bible talks about it: being enticed to improper, sinful behavior. It's important to know that facing temptation is not sin. Giving in to temptation is the sin. Temptation has been around since God placed Adam and Eve in the Garden of Eden. Scripture says that Satan tempted Adam and Eve to eat the fruit of the tree of the knowledge of good and evil with the promise that they would be like God. Potiphar's wife sexually tempted Joseph. David was tempted with a clear opportunity to kill King Saul in the caves of En-Gedi. Satan tempted Jesus to turn stones into bread when He was hungry in the wilderness. Greed tempted Ananias and Sapphira to hold back a part of the proceeds from the sale of their property.

Temptation comes in these forms and many others, and we each have our own area of weakness. Maybe you've faced the temptation to fudge your expense report, or take something that's not yours, or cheat on your tax return. Many of us have had to fight the urge to glance at something we shouldn't be looking at on the internet, flirt with someone outside of our marriage, take credit for someone else's work, seek the praise of men, worship idols, and on and on. Temptation confronts us in many ways every single day. It's so prevalent that we can grow numb to it to the extent that we give in to it without even putting up a fight. Soon enough, the sin that results from temptation becomes a habit! It would be helpful to know where it comes from and how to handle it when we face it.

## WHERE DOES TEMPTATION COME FROM?

Temptation comes from the fact that we have sin natures that lure us toward sin. Consistent with human nature that refuses to accept accountability for our sin, we tend to want to blame someone else when we succumb to temptation. Let's get one thing straight...

### *TEMPTATION IS NOT FROM GOD*

Temptation comes from within us and outside of us, but it does not come from God. It is common today to blame God when we fall into temptation. The reasoning is: "God made me this way, so it's His fault that I am addicted to pornography, alcohol, drugs, food, money, sex, power, etc." The Bible is clear that temptation does not come from God. James wrote, "Let no one say when he is tempted, 'I am being tempted by God'; for God cannot be tempted by evil, and He Himself does not tempt anyone" (James 1:13). We may ask, then, If God doesn't tempt anyone, doesn't He at least bear some responsibility for creating us with the ability to choose evil over good? After all, what chance do we have to avoid sin when it's so enticing, and God made us susceptible to its attraction?

God is not responsible for our sinful choices. God made us with a moral compass, with an innate ability to know right from wrong and to choose accordingly. We alone bear responsibility for our actions. That's why the Bible says repeatedly, that though God is sovereign, we are moral free agents, responsible for our choices. Take Deuteronomy 27-30, for example. God had just laid out His entire law for Moses. God told Moses, and Moses told the people what God expected of them. Moses said that God would curse them for disobedience and bless them for their obedience. Then God said:

> See, I have set before you today life and prosperity, and death and adversity; in that I command you today to love the Lord your God, to walk in His ways and to keep His commandments and His statutes and His judgments, that you may live and multiply, and that the Lord your God may bless you in the land where you are entering to possess it. But if your heart turns away and you will not obey, but are drawn away and worship other gods and serve them, I declare to you today that you shall surely perish. You will not prolong *your* days in the land where you are crossing the Jordan to enter and possess it. I call heaven and earth to witness against you today, that I have set before you life and death, the blessing and the curse. So choose life in order that you may live, you and your descendants, by loving the Lord your God, by obeying His voice, and by holding fast to Him; for this is your life and the length of your days, that you may live in the land which the Lord swore to your fathers, to Abraham, Isaac, and Jacob, to give them (Deut. 30:15-20).

God gave them a real choice: blessings for obedience, curses for disobedience. He implored them to *choose* life, but the decision and responsibility was theirs. God does not bear responsibility for our poor choices. The blame lies with us. Let's think more about temptation from the book of James.

. . .

## WE ARE RESPONSIBLE

James emphatically declared that we are responsible for our temptation, and the consequences when we fail. "But each one is tempted when he is carried away and enticed by his own lust. Then when lust has conceived, it gives birth to sin; and when sin is accomplished, it brings forth death" (James 1:14-15). James stressed that temptation does not come from God, but from our wicked desires. Let's look at some other scriptures that describe this sin nature within us that tempts us and causes us to make bad choices.

In the famous passage where Jesus told His apostles to cut off their hands or gouge out their eyes if they were causing sin, Jesus was attributing the problem of sin to the members of our body, and our inherently wicked desires (see Matt. 5:29-30).

In the equally famous passage in Romans 7 where Paul recounts his own struggle with sin, "the good that I want, I do not do, but I practice the very evil that I do not want," he recognized that he was responsible and accountable for the sin in his life (see Rom. 7:18-23).

God does not give us a pass for our sin. Nor can we get off the hook by shifting the blame on to someone else. Our sins are our fault. We are responsible not to yield to temptation, and we are culpable when we fail.

## SATAN TEMPTS US

Our sinful desires cause our temptation and sin, but we are not alone in this. Satan knows that we are sinful creatures, susceptible to temptation and sin. He wants to destroy us. He knows our propensity to sin and does all he can to be sure that we will fail. That's why we must remain ever mindful that Satan works evil in the world. Peter reminds us, "Be of sober spirit, be on the alert. Your adversary, the devil, prowls around like a roaring lion, seeking someone to devour" (1 Peter 5:8). Satan is not omniscient, but he does know our weaknesses. He tempts us in diverse ways depending on our predisposition to certain sins. I am susceptible to worry. Satan triggers things in my mind to fret about all the time. I constantly battle that temptation. Worry may not be your issue, but you have your own struggles. You have temptations that I don't have, but Satan knows them, and he uses them to try to crush you. Sometimes, Satan is successful. Let's look at him in action.

The very first sin in the Bible happened in the Garden of Eden. God created Adam, placed him in the garden and gave him dominion over everything in it. God restricted Adam in only one way. God told Adam, "From any tree of the garden you may eat freely; but from the tree of the knowledge of good and evil you shall not eat, for in the day that you eat from it you will surely die" (Gen. 2:16-17). After placing Adam there, God decided that, even though Eden met Adam's every need, it was "not good for man to be alone." So, God created Eve. They lived in perfect peace with God and with each other. The Bible says they were "naked and unashamed." Enter Satan.

Now the serpent was more crafty than any beast of the field which the Lord God had made. And he said to the woman, "Indeed, has God said, 'You shall not eat from any tree of the garden?'" The woman said to the serpent, "From the fruit of the trees of the garden we may eat; but from the fruit of the tree which is in the middle of the garden, God has said, 'You shall not eat from it or touch it, or you will die.'" The serpent said to the woman, "You surely will not die! For God knows that in the day you eat from it your eyes will be opened, and you will be like God, knowing good and evil." When the woman saw that the tree was good for food, and that it was a delight to the eyes, and that the tree was desirable to make one wise, she took from its fruit and ate; and she gave also to her husband with her, and he ate. Then the eyes of both of them were opened, and they knew that they were naked; and they sewed fig leaves together and made themselves loin coverings (Gen. 3:1-7).

Notice how Satan tempted Eve. His strategy was to cause her to question what God had said. Satan asked, "Has God said?" Eve said we can't eat it *or touch it* or we will die. If you read the passage closely, you'll see that God never said anything about touching the fruit. But Satan knew that if he could make Eve look at it, think about it, and hold it, she would eat it.

Next Satan questioned God's judgment against them if they did eat the fruit. Satan scoffed, "You surely will not die." That was a half-truth, which is still a lie. They *would* die, just not immediately. Then Satan questioned God's goodness and character. He suggested that God was holding back His best by setting unfair restrictions. Satan drove the nail home by questioning God's motives. "God knows that on the day you eat of it, your eyes will be opened and you will be like God." Wow! Imagine the temptation to be like God. It was more than Eve could take. The fruit looked so good, and it could make her wise. Who could resist? Not Eve. She took the fruit and ate, and she gave some to Adam and he ate too.

Satan tricked Eve. He enticed her to sin by causing her to want more for herself than God had already provided. Satan planted the seed and Adam and Eve chose to mistrust God. When she ate, Satan won a great battle. Sin and death entered the world. When God passed judgment on them, God did not tolerate Adam's attempt to blame Him. Adam said, "The woman whom YOU gave to be with me, she gave me from the tree, and I ate" (Gen. 3:12 emphasis added). Nor did God accept Eve's attempt to blame the serpent. Eve said, "The serpent deceived me, and I ate" (Gen. 3:13). God held Adam and Eve responsible for their sin and judged them for it. He cursed Satan too, but Satan gained his victory.

We need to recognize areas where we are vulnerable to temptation, and the reasons why. Temptation is often the result of our dissatisfaction with God's provision. When we think God has withheld something from us that we believe we deserve, such as that raise or promotion we wanted, or when we believe that God has withheld His best, we will grumble against Him. We may focus on the one thing He has not given, rather than finding satisfaction in all that He has provided. Temptation may lead us to seize for ourselves what God hasn't chosen to give. Desire to have the one thing we lack is extremely powerful. It's the cause of most of our sins. Satan knows where he can tempt us to feel disillusioned, and he does all he can to push us down the path toward sin.

We can resist Satan though. Remember in Matthew 4, right after John baptized Jesus, the Spirit led Jesus into the wilderness so Satan could tempt Him. After fasting forty days and forty nights, Jesus became hungry. Satan came and said to him, "If you are the Son of God, tell these stones to become bread." Jesus didn't need to prove to Satan that He was the Son of God. They both knew full well that He was. Satan tempted Jesus to use His divine power for His benefit in a way that would disobey God's plans. Jesus said, "It is written, Man shall not live on bread alone but on every word that proceeds from the mouth of God." For Jesus, what came from God's mouth was more important than what entered His mouth. Food is fleeting.

When that effort failed, in Matthew 4:5-7, Satan quoted Psalm 91:11-12 to Jesus, but he twisted it to persuade Jesus to jump from the highest peak of the temple. He said to Jesus, "If You are the Son of God, throw Yourself down; for it is written, 'He will command His angels concerning You;' And, 'On their hands they will bear You up, So that You will not strike Your foot against a stone.'"

But Jesus answered Satan with scripture, Jesus said to him, "On the other hand, it is written, 'You shall not put the Lord your God to the test.'" The word of God endures forever. It is wise for us to memorize as much of it as we can to help us avoid Satan's overtures.

You may say, "Okay, Jesus succeeded where Adam and Eve failed, but Jesus was God, that's an unfair advantage." Fair enough. The lesson for us is that Jesus knew the word of God and wanted to obey. If we valued the word of God and obedience to His will as Jesus did, we would not be sinless, but we would sin less.

Let's consider the case of Joseph, Jacob's son. He was fully human, with no advantage of deity. Joseph's brothers sold him into slavery, and he became a steward in the house of a wealthy man named Potiphar. Potiphar quickly realized that Joseph was special because everything he touched prospered. So, Potiphar made Joseph head over everything in his household. But Joseph was a handsome young man, and Potiphar's wife noticed him and made bold sexual advances toward him. Joseph pleaded with her, "Behold, with me here, my master does not concern himself with anything in the house, and he has put all that he owns in my charge. There is no one greater in this house than I, and he has withheld nothing from me except you, because you are his wife. How then could I do this great evil and sin against God?" (Gen. 39:8-9).

Potiphar's wife was not the kind of woman who took no for an answer. One day, she aggressively begged Joseph to sleep with her. He ran out of the house with her still clutching his outer garment. Humiliated, Potiphar's wife cried out for help, accusing Joseph of attempting to "make sport" of her, a euphemism for rape. Potiphar had him arrested and thrown in an Egyptian prison where he remained for years until God rescued him. Joseph did not fall victim to temptation, even though it cost him his position in Potiphar's house and landed him in jail. Joseph had his priorities in proper order. He loved God even though his life had not turned out as he had hoped, and he also had a sense of duty and loyalty to Potiphar. Joseph met her unsolicited advances by telling her that lying with her was wrong. It was a sin against Potiphar and against God. When that didn't work, Joseph had a Plan B: Run like crazy!

## HOW DO WE HANDLE TEMPTATION?

What do we do when we face difficult and various temptations? Some battle same-sex attraction. Pornography tempts others. Others consider beginning an adulterous relationship, either emotional, physical or both. Food is a strong draw for some. Alcohol, drugs, or theft tempt some, while a craving for power or admiration enamors others. The sin is not in the enticement, but when we give in to it. Martin Luther is credited with saying, "You can't stop the birds from flying over your head, but you can stop them from nesting in your hair."[1] How can we stop the birds from nesting in our hair?

. . .

### Go to Jesus, who sympathizes with us in our weakness

The writer of Hebrews reminds us: "For we do not have a high priest who cannot sympathize with our weaknesses, but One [Jesus] who has been **tempted in all things** as we are, yet without sin. Therefore let us draw near with confidence to the throne of grace, so that we may receive mercy and find grace to help in time of need" (Heb. 4:15-16, emphasis added).

For Jesus to be able to be our guide and our light, and for us to be able to receive mercy from Him and find grace in our time of need, He had to face temptation in every way that we do. Think about it like this. If you need counseling because of drug abuse, alcoholism, pornography, or same-sex attraction, you want to talk to someone who has experienced what you are experiencing. Who better to talk to than one who has already learned how to cope with the same temptations you have? Everyone has experienced temptation. Jesus experienced temptation in *all* things. We can go to Him with anything and everything because He has experienced every category of temptation. That's how He's able to be our help in time of need.

But how has Jesus experienced temptation in *all things*? We should understand that whether Jesus was tempted is not the debate. Satan *did* tempt Jesus. The debate that has raged for 2000 years is not whether Jesus could be tempted, but whether Jesus could have sinned. The argument goes, if Jesus couldn't sin, then His temptation wouldn't be true temptation. Theologians call the doctrine that Jesus could not sin, *impeccability*. William G.T. Shedd explained the solution to the problem as follows:

> A person who cannot sin, it is said, cannot be tempted to sin. This is not correct any more than it would be correct to say that because an army cannot be conquered, it cannot be attacked.

Temptability depends on the constitutional *susceptibility* while impeccability depends on the *will*. Those temptations were very strong but if the self-determination of his holy will was stronger than they, then they could not induce Him to sin and he would be impeccable. And yet he would be plainly temptable.[2]

To say it more simply, Jesus was fully God and fully man. He had two desires (divine and human), but His divine desire controlled His human desire. His human desire always obeyed His divine desire. For example, in the Garden of Gethsemane, Jesus, in His humanity, desperately wanted to avoid the cross. Yet in His Deity, He was completely submissive to His Father's will. His Deity controlled His human desires.

Well, if He couldn't sin, then how could He be tempted in all things? Charles Ryrie wrote, "All sinful desires can be classified as either lusts of the flesh, lusts of the eyes, or the boasting of possessions (or a combination thereof, 1 John 2:16). The tests that Satan put the Lord through fall into those three categories."[3] The trial Jesus experienced in the Garden was greater than any we will ever experience, but Jesus submitted to His Father's will. There has never been such spiritual anguish before or since. How much temptation Jesus must have experienced to avoid the cross, or to come down from the cross while He endured God's wrath! Jesus did not face the identical trials we do. For example, Jesus did not have to deal with internet pornography or a fast-food restaurant on every corner. However, the temptations He confronted were representative of every kind of temptation.

As God, Jesus is omniscient. He knows everything, so He understands our temptations better than we do. The temptations He met were real and worse than anything we have ever experienced. Thomas Lea described it this way: "Because Jesus never yielded to sin, we know that he faced more intense temptation. Most of us say 'yes' to sin before Satan has thrown all his weapons of temptation at us. Jesus said 'no' as Satan hurled every arrow in his quiver."[4] And notice this: Hebrews 4:15 says that Jesus was tempted so that He could *sympathize* with us. We can't be sinless like Jesus, but Jesus knows what it is like to face temptation, and He wants to help us through it. Jesus can sympathize with us and help us when we need it.

How do we avail ourselves of this help? We go to Him. We fall on our knees before Him and pray with all our might that we might not fall victim to the temptations that can ensnare us.

People who wrestle with same-sex attraction must rely on Him every minute. So do addicts to food, drugs, alcohol, and pornography. It doesn't matter what the addiction, the struggle is ever-present in an addict's life. Jesus promised in John 14 that He would send a helper, the Holy Spirit:

"But the Helper, the Holy Spirit, whom the Father will send in My name, He will teach you all things, and bring to your remembrance all that I said to you. Peace I leave with you; *My peace I give to you*; not as the world gives do I give to you. *Do not let your heart be troubled*, nor let it be fearful" (John 14:26-27, emphasis added).

Jesus gives us peace through the power of the Holy Spirit. The power and draw of temptation is the opposite of peace. Temptation creates inner turmoil. It's the opposite of an untroubled heart. Jesus promised that the Spirit could give us real peace. It takes constant reliance on Jesus, the power of the Holy Spirit, and the power of prayer. By God's grace, over time we will be less tempted by these things, and one day we may even be able to be free of their allure altogether. This is demanding work. It's painful work. But we can rely on Jesus to help us when we have need.

### PATTERN YOUR LIFE AFTER THE SUCCESSES OF OTHERS

David was not a perfect person. He failed spectacularly more than once. But he also brilliantly succeeded sometimes too. We shouldn't pattern our lives after the whole person of David, but we can model his successes. David had been on the run from Saul, hiding in caves from him for twenty years. One day, needing to relieve himself, Saul entered the very cave where David was hiding. It was a perfect opportunity for David to kill Saul and become king as God had promised years ago. After twenty years on the run from Saul, who could have blamed him? Even his men encouraged him to do it. He surely considered it. But then he conquered his desire. He refused to lay a hand on the Lord's anointed. Instead, David cut off a piece of Saul's garment to show the king that he had spared his life.

How was David able to succeed? He wasn't thinking about himself and what he wanted. He was thinking about what God wanted and doing things God's way. He knew that God had anointed him king, and God would bring it to pass in His perfect timing. For all his failures, this was a dramatic success. He could have tried to speed God's plan along by giving in to the temptation to take matters into his own hands. Instead, he waited and allowed God's plan to unfold in God's timing.

We will never have the opportunity to kill the king so we can fill his seat. But imagine you've been waiting for a big promotion, but you're competing with someone who you know has behaved unethically toward the company. Do you go to the boss and report the conduct, or do you let God handle it? We may want the promotion and the raise that comes with it so badly that we don't exercise the patience that David showed. I think that if David were in that situation, he would let God handle it. God has a way of doing the right thing in His own timing. Pattern your life and responses to temptation after David's patience, and trust in God's timing.

## PREPARE AN ESCAPE PLAN BEFORE YOU NEED IT

How did Joseph succeed where so many of us fail? Often, we're unprepared for how we will respond to temptation when we face it. Joseph had a plan. If words didn't work, his feet would carry him away from temptation. Jesus was able to answer Satan because He had memorized scripture and applied it when tempted.

The most famous verse in the Bible on how to avoid temptation is: "No temptation has overtaken you, but such as is common to man; and God is faithful, who will not allow you to be tempted beyond what you are able, but with the temptation will provide the way of escape also, so that you will be able to endure it" (1 Cor. 10:13). This verse is a promise from God. He will always give you a way to escape. There are many ways to flee from temptation. You are not a victim. Don't accept your sin as though it's an unchangeable part of your DNA. God may be using temptation in your life to cause you to depend on Him. You have the strength in you, by the power of the Holy Spirit, to change.

Sin is often the result of not having developed an escape plan for the temptations that we are likely to face. When I used to work as an attorney, overbilling my clients was a constant temptation. I felt enormous and relentless pressure to meet billing goals to justify my worth. I billed by the hour, and who would ever know if I added a tenth of an hour here or a quarter of an hour there? Because I knew this temptation was very real and difficult for me, I changed my billing structure. Whenever possible, I billed on a flat fee basis instead of an hourly basis. That solved 90% of my problems. If you don't recognize the areas of your life where you are likely to fall victim to temptation and develop a plan to combat that temptation, you've already lost the battle. Satan's got you, and you will fail. When you have prepared in advance how you will handle that temptation, you will be more likely to succeed. Not having an escape plan before you face the temptation exponentially increases your chances that you will fall into sin.

## CONCLUSION

Now about that astronomy test. I must have picked the wrong kid to cheat from because I got a D on the test, and a D in the class! I'm not sure if I would have made a D on my own or not, so in a sense I was grateful, but the moral of the story is that if you are going to cheat on your test, pick a smart kid to cheat from. I'm kidding! Actually, that's not the moral of the story at all. The moral of the story is to be prepared in all circumstances, knowing that temptation to sin will be present in almost every situation. When we face it in all its potential forms, remember that Jesus has suffered temptation in all things and that we can go to Him for help. Adam and Eve couldn't resist temptation, and their sin introduced the sin nature into humanity. Joseph and David were sinful humans, and they yielded to temptation sometimes, but when they succeeded, it was because they were modeling God's character. Don't follow their sin but emulate their successes that reflect God's character and provision. Wait on God's timing like David. Have a plan of escape before you need it like Joseph. Pray like crazy when you are staring down temptation. Go to Jesus with every temptation.

The old hymn by Annie S. Hawks and Robert Lowry, "I Need Thee Every Hour," says it like this:

> I need Thee every hour,
> Stay Thou near-by;
> Temptations lose their power,
> When Thou art nigh.[5]

# 6

# GUILT AND SHAME

**"There is therefore no condemnation for those
who are in Christ Jesus" Romans 8:1**

I was 17 years old, a senior in high school, and I had a gambling problem. I used to like to go to the racetrack and bet on horses. (I know that's illegal, but it was before I was a Christian!) I struck up a friendship with one of the tellers who takes the bets. He had his ear on the ground, so to speak, and sometimes would give me information that bettors call tips. He had a tip on a horse running the next night. The horse had been training well according to his trainer and was ready to break through. Unfortunately for me, as a 17-year-old, I didn't have enough money to make a significant bet.

Here's where the story goes south. I knew that my father kept an old cigar box in his dresser with some cash in it. It was really very simple. I would borrow $100 from my father, place the bet, collect the winnings, and return the $100 before he noticed that it was missing. What could go wrong? My horse was in the lead the whole race, until the top of the stretch. (That's the final straightaway.) At this racetrack, it was usually not good to be leading at the top of the stretch. It's a long straightaway to the finish line. My horse had broken the wind for the trailing horses, and they were fresher and well-positioned to overtake him down the stretch. My horse held up until about halfway down the stretch before other horses raced past him. He finished fourth.

I remember the pit in my stomach as I watched my horse fall behind. I knew it was over with 100 yards to go. I screamed at the top of my lungs, threw my race program, and tore up my ticket. I just lost my father's $100. That may not seem like a lot of money now, but for a 17-year-old paper boy in 1983, it was. I needed to replace that money quickly, but I had no means. Unfortunately for me, while I schemed to replace the money, my father noticed that it was gone. My parents brought me into their room to question me about the missing money. They asked if I thought that any of my four younger brothers might have taken it. I don't know to this day if they really thought that one of my brothers had taken the money, or if they used that technique to force my confession. Well, I did confess. I'll never forget my parents crumbling in heartbreak and disappointment when I told them the truth. It's horrible to hurt and disappoint your parents. I was guilty of the crime and wracked with shame. I don't know how many years it took to regain their trust.

## THE MEANING OF GUILT AND SHAME

We often use the words guilt and shame interchangeably, but there is a difference in the Bible. Guilt is objective. When you commit a crime or a sin, you ARE guilty of it, whether you feel guilty about it or not. We often use the word guilt subjectively, as in, "I feel so guilty about what I did." That's proper usage of the word guilt according to our dictionaries, but the Bible never uses it that way. The word *guilt* or *guilty, avon* or *asham* in the Hebrew scriptures, and *anokos* in Greek, appears about 135 times, and it never means *feelings* of guilt. It means objective guilt.

Not surprisingly, many of those uses are in the first five books of the Bible, after Moses received the law from God, and God instituted the sacrificial system to atone for the guilt of sin. Whenever someone was objectively guilty of a sin, God required a guilt offering, typically the sacrifice of a bull or a goat. God removed the person's judicial, objective guilt, because of the sacrifice, and the person returned to his or her life. The word means objective guilt in the New Testament, too. "Therefore whoever eats the bread or drinks the cup of the Lord in an unworthy manner, **shall be guilty** of the body and the blood of the Lord" (1 Cor. 11:27 emphasis added. See also Mark 3:29, Matt. 5:22, Luke 23:4).

Shame is a subjective feeling that may result from guilt. The Old Testament most often uses the Hebrew word *bosh* to describe shame. "O my God, I am ashamed and embarrassed to lift up my face to You, my God, for our iniquities have risen above our heads and our guilt has grown even to the heavens" (Ezra 9:6). The guilt of the people caused Ezra's shame.

The New Testament word used most frequently to describe shame is *aiskuno*. It means to feel shame, to have a sense of shame, or to be ashamed. "Therefore what benefit were you then deriving from the things of which you are now *ashamed*?" (Romans 6:21, emphasis added). Paul's audience felt shame over its past sins.

. . .

IN THE BIBLE, GUILT IS FACTUAL AND OBJECTIVE. SHAME IS A subjective feeling that may result from guilt. In my case, I was objectively guilty of stealing from my parents. I had committed the crime. The feeling I felt was such a crushing shame that I couldn't look them in the eyes or be in the same room with them. My father worked so hard, and I couldn't believe that I was such a lowlife that I would steal his money and gamble it away at the track. What a loser!

A close cousin to shame is *remorse*. The Greek word is *metamelomi* which means, "to have regrets about something in the sense that one wishes it could be undone."[1] "Then when Judas, who had betrayed Him, saw that He had been condemned, he felt *remorse* and returned the thirty pieces of silver to the chief priests and elders, saying, 'I have sinned by betraying innocent blood'" (Matt. 27:3-4 emphasis added).

The removal of guilt and shame requires more than just expressing remorse. Judas was guilty of betraying innocent blood, and he expressed remorse by going to the priests to try to undo what he had done. Removing guilt requires repentance, confession, and asking for forgiveness. To *repent* means to turn away from something, to change your mind about something. If we want God to cleanse us of our guilt before Him, and the guilt, shame, and remorse that we feel, we must confess our sin and repent of it. When we repent from our sin, God forgives us and removes the objective guilt of our sin. It's then up to us to leave behind the shame that we feel.

\* \* \*

## A BIBLICAL EXAMPLE OF GUILT AND SHAME: DAVID AND BATHSHEBA

Let's look at David's sin with Bathsheba to see how God convicted him of sin, which led him to shame, remorse, confession, and repentance. The story begins in 2 Samuel 11.

### THE CRIME

> Then it happened in the spring, at the time when kings go out to battle, that David sent Joab and his servants with him and all Israel, and they destroyed the sons of Ammon and besieged Rabbah. But David stayed at Jerusalem. Now when evening came David arose from his bed and walked around on the roof of the king's house, and from the roof he saw a woman bathing; and the woman was very beautiful in appearance. So David sent and inquired about the woman. And one said, "Is this not Bathsheba, the daughter of Eliam, the wife of Uriah the Hittite?" David sent messengers and took her, and when she came to him, he lay with her; and when she had purified herself from her uncleanness, she returned to her house. The woman conceived; and she sent and told David, and said, "I am pregnant" (2 Sam 11:1-5).

David should have been at the battle with his men, but instead was relaxing in his palace. He was where he shouldn't have been and seeing things he shouldn't have seen. He saw Bathsheba and wanted to take her for his own, though she was already married to Uriah the Hittite. It was bad enough that he took her, but when Bathsheba became pregnant, David had a real problem on his hands. Uriah was at the battle. Once

Bathsheba's pregnancy became obvious, simple math would tell Uriah that he was not the child's father. David needed Uriah to come home from the battle and sleep with Bathsheba to cover up his crime. He summoned Uriah home for some much-needed R&R. David ordered him to go down to his house. But Uriah slept at the king's door and would not go in to Bathsheba to eat and drink and have relations with her while his comrades were fighting. He showed far greater character than David.

## THE COVER UP

David thought his plot would work, but Uriah foiled it because of his integrity. David needed a new plan. He sent a letter to his general Joab, telling him to position Uriah on the front line and have everyone else step back. If Uriah died, David could take Bathsheba lawfully, but time was ticking. Uriah had to die quickly so the timing of Bathsheba's pregnancy would not be suspicious. Joab reported back to David that Uriah had indeed died in the battle. When the time of mourning was over, David sent and brought Bathsheba to his house, and she became his wife. So far, so good it seemed. Only David and Joab knew of the wicked plot. And God.

## THE VERDICT: GUILTY!

In 2 Samuel 12, God sent the prophet Nathan to tell David a little story:

> "There were two men in one city, the one rich and the other poor. The rich man had a great many flocks and herds. But the poor man had nothing except one little ewe lamb, which he bought and nourished; and it grew up together with him and

his children. It would eat of his bread and drink of his cup and lie in his bosom, and was like a daughter to him. Now a traveler came to the rich man, And he was unwilling to take from his own flock or his own herd, To prepare for the wayfarer who had come to him; Rather he took the poor man's ewe lamb and prepared it for the man who had come to him" (2 Sam. 12:1-4).

David was appalled at the selfishness of the rich man and declared that this man deserved to die. He must make restitution for the lamb times four, because he did this thing with no compassion. David was very slow to catch on, so Nathan said to David, "You are that man!" Imagine David's horror as he realized that Nathan knew about his sin and exposed it to him. God declared David objectively guilty of sin. He was not only an adulterer, but a murderer and a liar. God's punishment:

Now therefore, the sword shall never depart from your house, because you have despised Me and have taken the wife of Uriah the Hittite to be your wife.' Thus says the Lord, 'Behold, I will raise up evil against you from your own household; I will even take your wives before your eyes and give *them* to your companion, and he will lie with your wives in broad daylight. Indeed you did it secretly, but I will do this thing before all Israel, and under the sun'" (2 Sam. 12:10-12).

Those words broke David. Shame, that deep personal shame of knowing his own guilt, set in. He said, "I have sinned against the Lord." In a stunning display of God's grace and mercy, Nathan said to David, "The Lord has taken away your sin; you shall not die." Unfortunately for David and Bathsheba, David's punishment, in addition to the chaos that would exist in his house, was that the illegitimate child born of the sinful union would die. God forgave David's sin, but there were still grave consequences.

## A BIBLICAL MODEL FOR HANDLING GUILT: PSALM 51

David wrote Psalm 51 after Nathan's convicting visit. Psalm 51 gives us a Biblical pattern for what to do when we are guilty of sin and experience the shame of it. If we confess our sin, God will forgive us and remove our guilt, and He will take away our shame if we leave it with Him.

### A PLEA FOR FORGIVENESS (v. 1-2)

> Be gracious to me, O God, according to Your lovingkindness; According to the greatness of Your compassion blot out my transgressions. Wash me thoroughly from my iniquity, and cleanse me from my sin.

David asked the Lord to forgive his sin. Consider the magnitude of David's sin. He took Uriah's wife and had sex with her, more than likely against her will. When she became pregnant David tried to cover up the crime. When that failed, he orchestrated Uriah's death by putting him on the front line of the battle. How could David come before the Lord with that much blood on his hands? He had to come to the Lord confessing his sin, with humility, remorse, repentance and a plea for restoration and reconciliation with God. David wove all of this into the next several verses of the psalm.

. . .

## CONFESSION OF SIN (V. 3-6)

> For I know my transgressions, and my sin is ever before me.
> Against You, You only, I have sinned, and done what is evil in
> Your sight, so that You are justified when You speak, And
> blameless when You judge. Behold, I was brought forth in
> iniquity, and in sin my mother conceived me. Behold, You
> desire truth in the innermost being, and in the hidden part You
> will make me know wisdom.

We must confess our sin, and not just generally. We must
confess our specific sin and ask the Lord to forgive that sin.
David was right to say that he sinned against the Lord only. Sin
is a violation of God's law, so sin is first against Him. Then, sin
is against the people hurt by it, Uriah, Bathsheba, the son who
died, and David's household, from which the sword would
never depart. Sin has consequences to the sinner, and to the
ones offended, but sin is against the Lord before all others. We
need to examine our lives for sin. We must confess it to God to
be cleansed from the guilt of our sin against Him. We need to
confess our sin to those we've sinned against and ask their
forgiveness. Then we can be freed from the shame of our sin.

## REMORSE, REPENTANCE, AND RESTORATION (V. 7-12)

> Purify me with hyssop, and I shall be clean; Wash me, and I
> shall be whiter than snow. Make me to hear joy and gladness,
> Let the bones which You have broken rejoice. Hide Your face
> from my sins, and blot out all my iniquities. Create in me a
> clean heart, O God, and renew a steadfast spirit within me. Do
> not cast me away from Your presence, and do not take Your

Holy Spirit from me. Restore to me the joy of Your salvation, and sustain me with a willing spirit.

David asked God to blot out his iniquities, create in him a clean heart, and renew a steadfast spirit within him. His remorse led to repentance. He asked God to remove his guilt. He asked the Lord's forgiveness, and that the Lord reconcile David to Himself. This is the one thing, and the most important thing, that Judas did not do. Judas showed remorse for his crime, but he never repented of it, confessed it to God, and asked for forgiveness. David turned from his wicked ways and back toward God, prayed for God's restoration, and promised renewed commitment to serve God.

### RENEWED COMMITMENT TO SERVICE (V. 13-17)

Then I will teach transgressors Your ways, and sinners will be converted to You. Deliver me from bloodguiltiness, O God, the God of my salvation; Then my tongue will joyfully sing of Your righteousness. O Lord, open my lips, That my mouth may declare Your praise. For You do not delight in sacrifice, otherwise I would give it; You are not pleased with burnt offering. The sacrifices of God are a broken spirit; A broken and a contrite heart, O God, You will not despise.

David was heartbroken and contrite. David knew that he had wronged the Lord. It was only by God's grace that He could declare David not guilty, and not require him to pay the penalty of death. David was remorseful, repentant, and restored. But how is this just? How can God be just if He allows the guilty to go unpunished?

## HOW COULD GOD UPHOLD JUSTICE WITHOUT TAKING DAVID'S LIFE?

God's law required the death penalty for adultery. "If there is a man who commits adultery with another man's wife, one who commits adultery with his friend's wife, the adulterer and the adulteress shall surely be put to death" (Lev. 20:10). Numbers 35 says **seven times** that a murderer must be stoned to death. So how can God uphold the law and not punish the guilty at the same time? The answer is that *someone* had to pay the penalty for David's sin, it just wasn't David. It was Jesus.

Let's look at Philippians 2:6-8:

> He [Jesus] existed in the form of God, did not regard equality with God a thing to be grasped, but emptied Himself, taking the form of a bondservant, *and* being made in the likeness of men. Being found in appearance as a man, He humbled Himself by becoming obedient to the point of death, even death on a cross.

Philippians 2:6 begins some of the most profound teaching about Jesus in the entire Bible. Jesus "existed in the form of God." We must understand who Jesus is to comprehend how He could pay the penalty for sin that God required of David. The word *form* translates the Greek word *morphe*. English does not have its exact equivalent. The word *form* does not refer to shape or size, but rather, the outward expression of a person's inner nature. It doesn't mean Jesus resembled God physically. If he wanted to say that Jesus resembled God, Paul would have used the Greek word *schema*. *Schema* refers to outward physical appearance that can change without our nature changing. We can dye our hair, get a nose job, lose or gain weight, and we age.

That's a change of *schema*, not a change of *morphe*. A biblical example of the use of the word *schema* is 2 Cor 11:14, "Satan disguises (*schema*) himself as an angel of light." He changes his appearance, not his nature.

*Morphe* means something different. Some Biblical examples of this word are found in Phil. 3:10, "that I may know Him and the power of His resurrection and the fellowship of His sufferings, being conformed (*morphe*) to His death." *Morphe* is a change to the inner man, the very essence of his being. Notice the same thing in Galatians 4:19, "My children, with whom I labor until Christ is formed (*morphe*) in you." The best example is in Romans 12:2, because it uses both *morphe* and *schema* in the same verse. "Do not be conformed (*schema*) to the world, but be transformed (morphe) by the renewing of your mind." *Schema* changes the outward appearance. We can conform our behavior to the world, but God doesn't want us to do that. He wants us to be transformed (*morphe*) inwardly so we will not conform outwardly to the world.

Paul said in Philippians 2 that Jesus existed in the *morphe* of God, not in appearance, but the very essence of God in His being. He has existed eternally as God. This is some of the most exalting language about Jesus anywhere in the New Testament to proclaim Jesus' eternality and deity. It's what theologians call *high Christology*. Here are a few other verses that express Jesus' deity and eternality:

In the beginning was the Word and the Word was with God and the Word was God (John 1:1).

God, after He spoke long ago to the fathers in the prophets in many portions and in many ways, in these last days has spoken to us in His Son, whom He appointed heir of all things, through whom also He made the world. And He is the radiance of His glory and the exact representation of His nature, and upholds all things by the word of His power (Heb 1:1-3).

He is the image of the invisible God, the firstborn of all creation. For by Him all things were created, both in the heavens and on earth, visible and invisible, whether thrones or dominions or rulers or authorities—all things have been created through Him and for Him. He is before all things, and in Him all things hold together (Col. 1:15-17).

These passages and many others stress Jesus' eternality and deity. Jesus Christ is eternal and eternally God. If Jesus is not God, the consequences would be catastrophic to us. If Jesus is not eternally God, then He is a created being, inferior to God, and unable to satisfy God's wrath against sin.

But to be an acceptable sacrifice Jesus also had to be a human being, subject to temptations just like we are but without sin. God required a perfect sacrifice for sin. The sacrificial system God established under Moses required the sacrifice of a perfect one-year-old lamb to atone for sin. No lamb with spot or blemish would suffice. The same is true of whoever would make atonement for our sins and satisfy God's wrath against our sin. He had to be perfect. He had to be a lamb without blemish. And that's what Jesus was.

"For we do not have a high priest who cannot sympathize with our weaknesses, but One who has been tempted in all things as we are, **yet without sin**" (Heb. 4:15 emphasis added). The whole human person, mind, body, and soul needs cleansing from the guilt of sin. If Jesus wasn't fully man; if He didn't have a human body, mind, and spirit; then His death did not cleanse our bodies, minds, and souls of our sins. Qualified to serve as our substitute, He paid the penalty for our sin. "Being found in appearance as a man, He humbled Himself by becoming obedient to the point of death, even death on a cross" (Phil 2:8).

Jesus offered Himself once and for all as a sacrifice for our sins.

> For it was fitting for us to have such a high priest, holy, innocent, undefiled, separated from sinners and exalted above the heavens; who does not need daily, like those high priests, to offer up sacrifices, first for His own sins and then for the sins of the people, because this He did once for all when He offered up Himself (Hebrews 7:26-27).

Later, the writer of Hebrews says that after offering Himself as a sacrifice, Jesus sat down, indicating that His sacrifice was acceptable to God.

> Every priest stands daily ministering and offering time after time the same sacrifices, which can never take away sins; but He, having offered one sacrifice for sins for all time, sat down at the right hand of God, waiting from that time onward until His enemies be made a footstool for His feet. For by one offering He has perfected for all time those who are sanctified (Hebrews 10:11-14).

Jesus was born to die. At Christmas we celebrate the beginning of Jesus' life, which had His death as its central purpose. The reason for Christmas is the cross. The cross satisfied God's wrath for the sin of all mankind. David's, yours, and mine. In love and grace, God chose to satisfy His own wrath against us by pouring it out on Himself, through Jesus, instead of us. He died for us, in our place, to pay the penalty we owe for our sin. That's how God can uphold the law and not punish the guilty at the same time. Paul said it like this in 2 Corinthians 5:21: "He made Him who knew no sin to be sin on our behalf, so that we might become the righteousness of God in Him."

What an incredible Savior we have!

## HOW CAN WE ACCEPT GOD'S FORGIVENESS AND SHED GUILT AND SHAME?

David's act of contrition is instructive for us. But we must understand that David was a man of faith. God called David "a man after God's own heart" (see 1 Sam. 13:14), and that was before David committed these unspeakable sins, knowing that David would commit them. If we want God's forgiveness, we need to be people after God's own heart too. How do we do it?

### ACCEPT THE GOSPEL

None of what I have just written is of any value to remove your guilt and shame if you have not accepted the gospel. If you have not received Jesus as your Lord and Savior, you are still guilty of your sin against God, and you will incur God's wrath. "He who believes in the Son has eternal life; but he who does not obey the Son will not see life, but the wrath of God abides on him" (John 3:36). To receive His forgiveness, we must believe that Jesus died on the cross for our sins and rose from the dead. But that's all God demands of us to remove our guilt and shame. Once we have done that, He declares us not guilty. His sacrifice covers our sin. When God looks at us, He sees Jesus, perfect, blameless, and holy before Him. When we sin in the future, we confess it and repent of it to restore our right relationship and fellowship with God, but Jesus has already paid the price for that sin on the cross.

### WHAT ABOUT THIS SHAME I FEEL?

Even though we know that God has forgiven us, we still know what we have done. Our sins sometimes have terrible consequences for the ones we love, and we can't change them. David's sin had ramifications for his family for generations. When our sins hurt those we love, we feel such horrible shame. How do we live with shame? Better yet, how do we shed the feeling of shame?

We must apply God's standard of justice to ourselves. If God says we are not guilty, then it's up to us to accept that. When we continue to harbor shame, we are refusing to receive God's forgiveness. We are continuing to judge ourselves and holding on to the shame, even though God has judged us not guilty. When we refuse to release our guilt and shame, we are putting our sinful, imperfect selves in the judgment seat that only God occupies. We must accept that we are sinners; that's a fact. But we are *forgiven* sinners. It's impossible to live sinless lives, although we should sin less, and our sin should disturb us more.

Nevertheless, God says through Paul in Romans, "There is therefore now *no condemnation* for those who are in Christ Jesus" (Romans 8:1 emphasis added). That's my favorite verse in the Bible. No matter what we have done, because we have trusted in Jesus for the forgiveness of our sins, God does not condemn us. If God does not condemn us, we should not continue to condemn ourselves. Forgive yourself! Let it go. Accept God's grace. He has removed your guilt. Ask forgiveness from those you have hurt and release the shame that you feel.

When Jesus met the woman caught in adultery in John 8, He said to her, "Neither do I condemn you; go and sin no more" (John 8:11 NKJV). He wiped her slate clean. No guilt. No shame. When the prodigal son returned to his father, he began to recite his speech of remorse, confession, and repentance that he had practiced along the way. His father barely let him begin before he dressed him in the royal robe, put the signet ring on his finger, and threw a party in his honor (see Luke 15:11-32). No guilt. No shame. Don't judge yourself guilty when God has judged you not guilty. Don't carry the shame that Jesus died to remove on the cross. Bask in God's grace.

## CONCLUSION

When I stole from my father, I knew that I had wronged my parents and hurt them deeply. But it wasn't until I became a parent that I truly understood what I had done. Now that I'm a father, I know with greater clarity how much my sin hurt them. It wasn't the $100. It was the breach of trust, the disregard for how hard my father worked to earn money, the lack of appreciation for all he provided, the disrespect I showed. It was the gulf between my parent's love for me and the lack of love I showed them. It was their grief in raising a child who could do something like that. Before I was a father, I didn't know how much my parents loved me. Kids aren't capable of loving their parents like their parents love them. It's only when we love to infinity that we can be hurt to infinity. I'm sure that's how my parents felt that day.

I called my parents recently to ask them to forgive me for what I did. I should have done it in 1983, but better late than never. Would you believe that they didn't even remember it?

That's how much my parents love me, so much that they don't remember my sins against them.

That's how God loves His children too. We sin against Him and disrespect Him every day. We don't mean to, but we often take His provision for granted. We choose other gods over Him. We refuse to obey His will. Yet, He loves us to infinity. That's why He was willing to pay the infinite price of dying on the cross to pay for our sin so we wouldn't have to pay it ourselves. There's no greater love possible than that. He died for our sin and forgives us of it. Although God can't forget anything, He chooses to not remember our sin. It's covered by the blood of Jesus. Now if He was willing to pay that price to remove our guilt and shame from us and to forgive our sin, isn't it an insult to Him if we refuse to forgive ourselves and choose to hold on to our shame?

Elvina Hall expressed it like this in the lyrics to the song, "Jesus Paid it All":

> Jesus paid it all
> All to Him I owe
> Sin had left a crimson stain
> He washed it white as snow[2]

Jesus paid our sin debt in full. When God the Father looks at us, He sees the righteousness of His Son Jesus. Don't hold on to the shame that Jesus died to remove.

# 7

## MONEY

**For the love of money is the root of all
kinds of evil – 1 Timothy 6:10**

Molly and I currently have two kids in college. We both work in ministry, and money is tight. We often slip into conversations about how we are going to pay for this or that. I don't want to waste my time and energy fretting about money. A wise friend once said to me, "God will either choose to feed you or He won't." It's really that simple. God has never let me starve. He's never let me go a day without clothes on my back or a roof over my head. But that doesn't mean that one day He won't. Ideally, we would never focus on money, but on God who provides it. Deuteronomy reminds us: "You shall remember the Lord your God, for it is he who gives you power to get wealth" (Deut. 8:18, ESV). James, the Lord's brother wrote to the church, "Every good and perfect gift is from above" (James 1:17 NIV).

Money is a tool. It should be no different than a can opener. If we need to open a can, we take it out of the drawer. We don't feel any passion for the can opener. We use it to open the can, and then put it away and forget about it. But money is a different kind of tool. It's nearly impossible to be ambivalent about money. We worry if we have too little of it. How are we going to pay our bills, pay for college, or retire someday? We worry if we have too much of it. How are we going to protect it? Who's going to get it after we're gone and what will they do with it? Who's pretending to be our friend today because they want our money?

Our attitude toward money will determine whether it is a blessing or a curse on us. We will either be master over our money, or our money will be master over us. We must learn to put money in its proper place compared to the more essential things in life. In this chapter, we will look at how money can be a snare and how it can be a blessing. Let's look at an Old Testament and a New Testament example of someone for whom money became a curse.

## MONEY AS A CURSE

The love of money can cause a curse that lasts a lifetime as we will see from the life of Gehazi, Elisha's servant. It can even cost us our souls as we will see from Jesus' encounter with the rich young ruler.

### GEHAZI

In 2 Kings 5, Naaman was the commander of the army of the king of Aram, and he was a great man, but he had leprosy. Naaman heard that there was a prophet in Israel who could cure leprosy, so he came with an entourage to see Elisha. Elisha did not even come out to receive the great Naaman. Instead he sent a messenger to say to Naaman, "Go and immerse yourself in the Jordan River seven times and you will be healed." Naaman was angry at the personal slight, but his servants convinced him to comply, and he was healed. He returned to give gifts to Elisha, but Elisha wouldn't accept anything from him. Elisha said to him, "Go in peace." But Elisha had a servant named Gehazi who witnessed the whole exchange, and I want us to learn from his story.

After Naaman had traveled some distance,  Gehazi, the servant of Elisha the man of God, said to himself, "My master was too easy on Naaman, this Aramean, by not accepting from him what he brought. As surely as the Lord lives, I will run after him and get something from him." So Gehazi hurried after Naaman. When Naaman saw him running toward him, he got down from the chariot to meet him. "Is everything all right?" he asked. "Everything is all right," Gehazi answered. "My master sent me to say, 'Two young men from the company of the prophets have just come to me from the hill country of Ephraim. Please give them a talent of silver and two sets of clothing.'" "By all means, take two talents," said Naaman. He urged Gehazi to accept them, and then tied up the two talents of silver in two bags, with two sets of clothing. He gave them to two of his servants, and they carried them ahead of Gehazi. When Gehazi came to the hill, he took the things from the servants and put them away in the house. He sent the men away and they left (2 Kings 5:19-24 NIV).

Gehazi deceived Naaman into believing that Elisha had changed his mind. Naaman was happy to give two talents of silver, which equaled about seventy-five pounds of it. Gehazi loaded up his servants' donkeys with the money. Just before they returned to their village, Gehazi took the money from them and stashed it in his house. I don't know how he expected his crime to go undetected; people talk, especially when you don't even give them a cut! But such is the draw of money. Elisha knew all about what Gehazi had done.

> When he went in and stood before his master, Elisha asked him, "Where have you been, Gehazi?" "Your servant didn't go anywhere," Gehazi answered. But Elisha said to him, "Was not my spirit with you when the man got down from his chariot to meet you? Is this the time to take money or to accept clothes— or olive groves and vineyards, or flocks and herds, or male and female slaves? Naaman's leprosy will cling to you and to your descendants forever." Then Gehazi went from Elisha's presence and his skin was leprous—it had become as white as snow (2 Kings 5:25-27 NIV).

Lepers were separated from fellowship with the community and society because they were ceremonially unclean. Although Gehazi was not wealthy, as Elisha's servant, he had what he needed to live. But he was greedy. He wanted more, and as a result, he lost everything, and received the curse of leprosy too. The love of money can do that to us. For every person who ever hit it big in the stock market, there are many more who wanted to get rich quick, invested all their money in risky stocks, and lost their life savings.

But the love of money can cost us more than our personal wealth, it can cost us our souls. Jesus preached that where your treasure is, there your heart is also (Matt. 6:21), and that you cannot serve both God and money (Matt. 6:24). You will eventually have to choose between the two. You will love one and hate the other. Gehazi was a house divided against himself.

He worked for a servant of God, but his desire was for money. His eyes must have been as wide as saucers when he saw the wealth that Naaman offered Elisha and stunned when Elisha refused these gifts.

There is no evidence of an inner struggle in Gehazi's conscience. He wanted a portion of the gift and quickly devised a scheme to obtain it. God cursed Gehazi and his house with leprosy forever for his deceit. God demands that we love Him with all our heart, all our soul, all our minds and all our strength (Deut. 6:4). Jesus affirmed that this is the greatest commandment (Matt. 22:37). When we allow anything to become an idol, as Gehazi allowed money to become an idol, we replace God with something of infinitely less value. Consider an example from the New Testament.

## THE RICH YOUNG RULER

A certain ruler asked him [Jesus], "Good teacher, what must I do to inherit eternal life?" "Why do you call me good?" Jesus answered. "No one is good—except God alone. You know the commandments: 'You shall not commit adultery, you shall not murder, you shall not steal, you shall not give false testimony, honor your father and mother.'" "All these I have kept since I was a boy," he said. When Jesus heard this, he said to him, "You still lack one thing. Sell everything you have and give to the poor, and you will have treasure in heaven. Then come, follow me." When he heard this, he became very sad, because he was very wealthy. Jesus looked at him and said, "How hard it is for the rich to enter the kingdom of God! Indeed, it is easier for a camel to go through the eye of a needle than for someone who is rich to enter the kingdom of God" (Luke 18:18-25 NIV).

This man thought that he had earned the kingdom of heaven by his good works in keeping the law. Jesus quickly saw that his reliance on his works was a snare to him. To show him that he had not kept the law, nor could he, Jesus told him to part with the most important thing in his life, his money. Jesus showed him that he hadn't even kept the two most important commandments, to love God and to love others. Money was an idol in his life. He loved it more than anything. He had a choice to make. He chose his money and went away sad. He couldn't part with his wealth and it cost him the kingdom. Jesus' statement that it is easier for a camel to go through the eye of a needle than for a rich man to enter the kingdom of God stunned the apostles. They thought wealth equaled God's favor, so they asked,

"Who then can be saved?" Jesus replied, "What is impossible with man is possible with God." Peter said to him, "We have left all we had to follow you!" "Truly I tell you," Jesus said to them, "no one who has left home or wife or brothers or sisters or parents or children for the sake of the kingdom of God will fail to receive many times as much in this age, and in the age to come eternal life" (Luke 18:26-30 NIV).

Money is not the measure of the value of our lives. We need to be sure that we have believed the gospel of Jesus Christ, that He died for our sins and rose from the dead, and we need to help others do the same. What we do for the kingdom of God is the true measure of our lives' value. It's much more valuable than money. In fact, the Bible lists many other things that have more value than money.

## MORE VALUABLE THAN MONEY

It's often been said that money doesn't buy happiness. There have been many times when I have wanted to personally test that theory! But still, the good things in life can't be bought with money. Here are several treasures, some heavenly and some earthly, that money can't buy.


*Your Soul*

Jesus posed the question, "For what will it profit a man if he gains the whole world and forfeits his soul? Or what will a man give in exchange for his soul?" (Matt 16:26 ESV). Many people have spent their lives trying to accumulate as much money as they can. You may even be one of them. They want to take the most extravagant vacations, own the fanciest houses, and drive the most expensive sports cars. They make money an idol, allowing it to control their lives, constantly needing more of it so they can buy more of the stuff that they think makes them happy. All the while, they never give a thought to their eternal destiny. We will all come face to face with the prospect of death. Death is the ultimate leveler. Unless Christ returns first, we will all experience it. Death does not show favoritism to the rich. It comes for every one of us. When we confront death, it forces us to realize that no amount of money can buy our way out of it. There will come a time when we understand that money has been nothing but an obstacle to knowing God and serving Him. That's why Jesus remarked about the difficulty of a rich man entering the kingdom.

It reminds me of the rich man in Luke 16. He was wealthy, but cared nothing for poor Lazarus, the beggar at his gate who would eat the rich man's scraps. After the rich man died, it didn't matter one bit how much money he had during his life, he could not buy back his own soul. The beggar was in Abraham's bosom, and there was a great chasm fixed between the rich man and Lazarus. No amount of money could help the rich man traverse it.

Or what about the man in Luke 12 who was so wealthy that he had no place to store his crops?

> Then he said, 'This is what I will do: I will tear down my barns and build larger ones, and there I will store all my grain and my goods. And I will say to my soul, "Soul, you have many goods laid up for many years *to come*; take your ease, eat, drink *and* be merry."' But God said to him, 'You fool! This *very* night your soul is required of you; and *now* who will own what you have prepared?' (Luke 12:18-20).

No amount of money could buy back his soul, and the riches that he worked so hard in his life to accumulate went to someone else.

## Wisdom

> "Take my instruction and not silver, and knowledge rather than choicest gold. For wisdom is better than jewels; and all desirable things cannot compare with her" (Proverbs 8:10-11).

We acquire wisdom through reading the Bible, from the Holy Spirit, through instruction from others, and from life experience. Solomon constantly implored his son to get it at all costs during his life. Wisdom is the antidote to the trap of money. Advertisers bombard us with messages that we need this car, or that jewelry, or this appliance or that vacation to be happy. The wise man knows that he doesn't need any of those things to be happy. The Bible encourages us to live simple lives. Paul wrote that "the love of money is a root of all kinds of evil" (1 Tim. 6:10 NIV). Be wise. Don't love money; love God.

## LIFE

The love of money cost Ananias and Sapphira their lives in Acts 5. While people were selling their property and bringing the full price for the apostles to distribute to the poor, Ananias and Saphira were conspiring. They sold their property and agreed that they would deliver only part of the money to the apostles but keep the rest for themselves. They wanted people to give them credit and acclaim for their generosity, but they wanted it at a discount! It turned out to be their last and worst mistake. Peter asked them each separately, "Why has Satan filled your heart to lie to the Holy Spirit?" They both died, and the young men carried them out for burial.

## HEALTH

In Acts 3, Peter and John were walking up to the temple to pray and saw a lame man begging for money. Peter looked at him. The beggar made eye contact, expecting a monetary gift. Peter put the value of money in its proper relation to the man's health. He said to the lame beggar, "I do not possess silver and gold, but what I do have I give to you; In the name of Jesus Christ the Nazarene, walk!" (Acts 3:6). Money might feed this man for a day, but the ability to walk would be a blessing every day. We know our health is a greater blessing than money. Every time we spend money to join a gym or Weight Watchers, we're trading money for health. How many times have you heard people nearing their deaths say, "I'd give anything to feel better," or for a few more years? It's a request for health, and a realization that it is much more valuable than money.

### A GOOD MARRIAGE

"An excellent wife, who can find? For her worth is far above jewels" (Proverbs 31:10). I can testify to this one personally. You can't put a price tag on a good wife or a good marriage. Molly has been an incredible blessing in my life since we were teenagers, and even more so after we were married, and it gets better every year. When we hear about how others are struggling in their marriages, or are divorced or contemplating divorce for whatever reason, we remember how blessed we are. I wouldn't trade my marriage for all the money in the world. If you're a female reader, it is my prayer that you feel the same way about your husband. I pray he loves you as Christ loved the church (Eph. 5:25).

### CHILDREN

Like arrows in the hand of a warrior, So are the children of one's youth. How blessed is the man whose quiver is full of them" (Ps 127:4-5). Molly and I had infertility issues when we were trying to start a family. The doctors told us that we had about a 5% chance of having children, and even that window was closing fast. We didn't have much money, but we were willing to spend whatever we had to have children. When the doctor confirmed that Molly was pregnant with Allison after many procedures, we never once gave a thought to the money we had spent. What a blessing to be parents! When Brian came along naturally, that was just God showing off His power and generosity.

For whatever reason, God removed our infertility, where He didn't for others. I can't explain that, and I don't want to communicate that you can't have a full life without children. That's certainly not so. Our children have been a joy to us their whole lives and certainly more valuable than all the money in the world.

### A Good Reputation

"A good name is to be more desired than great wealth, Favor is better than silver and gold" (Prov. 22:1). Some people will do anything to become wealthy and stay wealthy, regardless of ethics or morality. The Enron and Madoff scandals are proof of that. Can you imagine money having such control over you that you would bankrupt old widows to have it? It happens every day. That's why we protect our identities so fiercely. People troll the internet for careless web surfers, to steal their identity, and then their money.

Ruth comes to mind when I think of a Biblical character who showed the value of a good reputation. She came to Israel from Moab with her mother-in-law Naomi after the death of her husband and Naomi's husband. Everyone in Jerusalem knew Naomi, because Naomi had lived there with her husband but left for Moab during a famine in Jerusalem. But Ruth was a stranger.

Ruth quickly earned a good reputation, first because she wouldn't abandon Naomi to return to Moab and her own people. Then she continued to increase her good stature by her work ethic and her humility.

. . .

BOAZ NOTICED HER. HE WANTED TO TAKE RUTH AS HIS WIFE, BUT there was a problem. Another man had the first right to marry her according to the laws of the day. If that man refused to marry her, then Boaz could. Boaz confronted this man in the public square and asked him if he would marry Ruth. He would not because he didn't want to dilute his children's inheritance. Boaz agreed to marry Ruth on the spot, in the presence of many witnesses.

With a good reputation, you can earn money. People will hire you, contract with you, buy from you, lend to you, and trust you enough so that money will *follow* your good reputation. With a bad reputation, just the opposite will happen. People will hear about you and run from you in matters of money.

You can lose money repeatedly and still earn it back. Many have done it. You can only lose your reputation once. Once it's gone, you can't get it back again. Protect your reputation over money.

## *TIME*

The less time we have, the more precious it becomes. In 2 Kings 20, King Hezekiah became ill. The prophet Isaiah relayed God's message that Hezekiah should put his house in order because he would not recover from this illness. Hezekiah wept bitterly over his impending death and prayed to God for more time. The Lord graciously healed him and granted him fifteen more years of life. When we face death, our money becomes worthless. Many people would trade everything for more time.

The list goes on and on of course. Money is valuable, but not more valuable than the things listed above. We should never sacrifice them for money. A person with a lot of money, but without these more essential blessings is a miserable person.

## HOW CAN MONEY BE A BLESSING INSTEAD OF A CURSE?

If God has chosen to bless you with excess resources, He has a reason for that. He doesn't intend for you to hoard your money. The more you guard it, the more you will think about it. The more you think about it, the more it has control over you, rather than you controlling it. So what do we do? Let me give you three general principles, followed by three specific suggestions for what we should do with our money.

### THREE GENERAL PRINCIPLES

These first three ideas are principles by which Christians should live their lives. I think you will find that if you adhere to them, you won't worry about money as much. The money you give will tend to find its way back to you.

### 1. BE A GOOD STEWARD

The most important principle is to hold on to your money loosely. At least one lesson of the Great Depression, and more recently, Covid-19, is that money is fleeting. It's a very tenuous thing to value. It can disappear quickly. Sometimes we lose money through no fault of our own. It's hard to predict a stock market crash. If you are heavily invested in the stock market, you may be an innocent victim of a crash, or you may be defrauded by a Bernie Madoff or an Enron scandal.

. . .

OTHER TIMES, GOD CAN CHOOSE TO TAKE WEALTH AWAY IF YOU'RE a poor steward of it. If you prove to be a good steward with the money that God has given you, He may choose to entrust you with more. Jesus taught about the principle of stewardship in the parable of the talents (Matthew 25:14-30). A man went on a journey but before he left, he entrusted one servant with five talents to invest, one servant with two talents, and a third servant with one talent. After a long time, the master returned to settle accounts with his servants. The servant who had been given five talents had earned five more. The servant who had received two talents earned another two. The master rewarded each of those servants by putting them both in charge of many more things.

But the servant who was given one talent did not invest it, but buried it, afraid that he might lose it. The master called him wicked and lazy, and took what the servant had from him. God intends for us to be good stewards with all that He provides. All the resources we have are gifts from God. A good steward understands that God owns all his resources and he is just managing the resources God has given. "The earth is the Lord's and everything in it, the world, and all who live in it" (Ps. 24:1 NIV). Recognize that you don't own what you have. It's God's, and only on loan to you.

## 2. BE ACCOUNTABLE TO GOD WITH HIS RESOURCES

Another principle that we learn from the parable of the talents is that God expects a return on His investment. It's not just that He may entrust us with more money if we demonstrate good stewardship over what He has given to us, although it's not less than that. I want to be a good steward over all the resources that God has given to me, because it's an honor if God should choose to trust me with more. I don't believe that God will continue to pour His resources into us if we are like a sieve that leaks those precious resources. But more than just the honor of being entrusted with more, one day He will demand an accounting for all of it.

I think of it like a mortgage with a bank. If you have good credit, the bank may give you a mortgage. Don't expect to be thanked when you pay your mortgage every first of the month. That's only what you are supposed to do. If you don't pay your mortgage, the bank will demand an accounting. That's called foreclosure! If you continue to be a good customer, the bank may entrust you with a car loan or a small business loan when you need it. The principle of a day of reckoning for bad stewardship applies to our relationship to the bank, and our relationship with God. God demands that we use well the resources given us. Invest what He has given you well, and on the day of accounting, you'll know that you have been a good steward of His resources.

### 3. *INVESTING IN THE KINGDOM IS INVESTING IN YOUR ETERNITY*

This is the principle of rewards. In the parable of the talents, the master rewarded the two stewards who doubled his money. The master said, "Well done, good and faithful servant! You have been faithful with a few things; I will put you in charge of many things. Come and share your master's happiness!" (Matthew 25:21, 23 NIV). Notice God blessed the two servants in both material and non-material ways. God put them in charge of many things, a material blessing, and invited them to share in their master's happiness, a non-material blessing. Someone once said that God cannot pour money or other blessings into a clenched fist. But into an open hand, He can pour many blessings. Be a cheerful giver (2 Cor. 8:9). "Honor the Lord from your wealth, and from the first of all your produce; So your barns will be filled with plenty. And your vats will overflow with new wine" (Prov. 3:9-10). Give to the Lord, and He will give back to you.

## Three Specific Suggestions

Now that we understand some basic principles of stewardship, I would like to offer some specific suggestions about what we can do with the resources God has entrusted to us.

### 1. Use your money to support your household

"If anyone does not provide for his own, and especially for those of his household, he has denied the faith and is worse than an unbeliever" ( 1 Tim. 5:8). This should be obvious, but most of us know people who have sunk into deep debt because they have spent their money on luxuries that they couldn't afford. They intended to provide for their families, but because of poor choices they failed. As a former lawyer, I have represented several clients who filed for bankruptcy because they mismanaged their money. I have also represented husbands in divorces who said that they would rather die than pay alimony or child support to their wives. So maybe this principle of using money to take care of your family is not as obvious as most of us might think.

When we read 1 Tim. 5:8, we might ask, "Who is our household?" Of course, we are going to take care of our own kids, but what about our aging parents? What about a brother or sister in need? What about an aunt, an uncle, or a cousin?

How far does *our household* extend? The word for household means, "persons who are related by kinship or circumstances and form a closely-knit group."[1]

Obviously, there is some gray area in that definition. Sometimes you need to make a judgment call about who your household includes, or about who genuinely needs help. Sometimes you'll have to decide who has real need, and who is lazy, or addicted to drugs or alcohol, and will only squander the money you give them. Try to be inclusive when drawing the lines. Be as generous as you can. Trust that God can replenish what you have given away.

### 2. USE YOUR MONEY TO HELP THE POOR

When Jesus preached the Sermon on the Mount, He assumed that people would give to the poor. His only concern was that people gave from proper motives. He said, "So *when* you give to the poor, do not sound a trumpet before you, as the hypocrites do in the synagogues and in the streets, so that they may be honored by men" (Matt. 6:2, emphasis added). Giving to the poor was not an *if*; it was a *when*. Jesus commanded giving to the poor in Luke 12. "Sell your possessions and give to charity; make yourselves money belts which do not wear out, an unfailing treasure in heaven, where no thief comes near nor moth destroys. For where your treasure is, there your heart will be also" (Luke 12:33-34).

What you do with your money says a lot about you. In solving crimes, detectives employ a tried and true principle to catch the perpetrator: Follow the money. Jesus said the same thing. Follow the money to find where your heart is. If you store your money in the bank or in "toys," you may have to examine your heart for selfishness. If you give your money to the poor, then that's proof that your heart is compassionate toward the less fortunate.

The first century church demonstrated this principle. "And all those who had believed were together and had all things in common; and they *began* selling their property and possessions and were sharing them with all, as anyone might have need" (Acts 2:44-45). Give to the poor as you are able. Poverty is a huge problem around the world, in America, and in your neighborhood. We can't fix it by ourselves, but we can help a little bit if we are willing to look for need. There are so many worthy causes and good organizations that support those causes. Stretch yourself and give a little more than you think you can afford. Watch God bless it.

### 3. USE YOUR MONEY TO BUILD GOD'S KINGDOM

The Book of Malachi reads like a courtroom scene with God as the prosecutor bringing indictment after indictment against the defendant, Israel. God charged Israel with robbing Him of the money needed to build the kingdom:

Will a man rob God? Yet you are robbing Me! But you say, 'How have we robbed You?' In tithes and offerings. You are cursed with a curse, for you are robbing Me, the whole nation *of you*! Bring the whole tithe into the storehouse, so that there may be food in My house, and test Me now in this," says the Lord of hosts, "if I will not open for you the windows of heaven and pour out for you a blessing until it overflows (Mal. 3:8-10).

That's the only time in the Bible where God commands anyone to test Him, and it's about our money. When we give to God, He can multiply it beyond what we can imagine. In the parable of the sower, the sower planted the seed in good soil, and God multiplied it 30 times, 60 times, and 100 times. Generosity toward the kingdom of God works the same way, even though we may not see the results until eternity.

So, don't rob God. Give to the church. Give also to His people. "So then, while we have opportunity, let us do good to all people, and especially to those who are of the household of the faith" (Gal 6:10).

## CONCLUSION

When is the last time you went an entire day without thinking about money? I don't know if I ever have. It's not necessarily a bad thing to think about money if you are thinking about it in a healthy way. Have a budget. Make sure the money coming in exceeds the money going out. If it doesn't, you must either increase your income or decrease your spending. Then, stick to that budget. When you have excess, be generous. Think about what even twenty dollars might mean to someone who is having a hard time making ends meet. Think about a single mom or dad who has to balance work with raising a family. Most people in that situation value a dollar more than those who have more money than they need. They have usually learned how to stretch twenty dollars as far as possible. There's a greater blessing in the giving of that $20 than the $20 could ever buy.

Sometimes the principle of input exceeding output won't work for a season. When our kids started college, we opened a line of credit on our house to draw from to help with tuition. We figured we'd be operating at a negative balance for a while, and we were willing to take on some debt for our kids that we love so much. It's part of the principle of sowing and reaping. We invest in our children now for blessing in the future. God says, the more you sow, the more you reap, as we learned from the parable of the sower and the parable of the talents above. It's never wrong to invest in our kids or in the kingdom of God.

As we have paid tuition bills over the past three and a half years, we have been continually amazed at what God has done. Somehow God has provided month after month so that we have not had to touch that line of credit for college. Just last semester, we learned that our daughter received $3,300.00 in financial aid that we didn't know was coming! God has shown us repeatedly that He can handle our finances even when we think that we can't possibly have enough. Sometimes it's in the lack that God shows Himself the most.

The fourth stanza of "Be Thou My Vision", says it like this:

> Riches I heed not, nor man's empty praise,
> thou mine inheritance, now and always:
> thou and thou only, first in my heart,
> High King of heaven, my treasure thou art.[2]

May God be the only ruler of our hearts, not money.

# 8

# COMPARISON

**"The Pharisee stood by himself and prayed: 'God, I thank you that I am not like other people—robbers, evildoers, adulterers—or even like this tax collector." Luke 18:11 (NIV)**

Comparison is not the same as competition, but they are related because comparison often leads to competition. Who has the most beautiful house, lawn, car, or TV? As a pastor, I have given up on being able to compare and compete with other people's stuff. I earn a good salary for a pastor, but I'll never be rich. As I said earlier, Molly also has a career in ministry, and with two kids in college, I can't compete on the material level with other people. I try not to spend any time comparing my stuff with theirs. I'm still not immune from the problem of comparison though. Instead of comparing portfolios, I might compare my pastoral and preaching abilities with others.

. . .

THE MOST SIGNIFICANT ROLE OF A PASTOR IS TO PREACH THE word so that the people will understand it and apply it to their lives. Every week I write and deliver a sermon to my congregation. Because I love the word of God and want to preach better all the time, I listen to a lot of sermons too. That's where the problem of comparison bites me most often. Some preachers preach without notes. I'm not able to do that. Others have much more scripture memorized than I do. Others are incredibly charismatic. If I allow myself to get into the comparison game, I start to feel insecure, inadequate, or ineffective. On and on it goes when we compare what we have with what others have.

Comparison is the thief of joy. When we compare *up*, we feel badly about ourselves. When we compare *down*, we become proud and judgmental. Most of the time, we compare up. I always compare myself to the best preachers, not those who have never delivered a sermon. Our kids compare themselves to friends whose parents gave them a Mustang for their sixteenth birthday, not the friends whose parents wouldn't let them date or have an iPhone until college. Social media has made things drastically worse. We can see in real time how others are vacationing in the Greek islands or baking amazing cakes, and everything in between.

## THE DANGERS OF COMPARISON

Comparison makes us think about ourselves more rather than less, which is the essence of pride. We will either feel bad about ourselves and wish we were like someone else when we compare up, or we will feel superior to someone else if we compare down. Comparison can lead us into all kinds of sin. Let's look at a few.

. . .

## SELF-EXALTATION

One of the great dangers of comparison is that we exalt ourselves. This is what happens when we compare "down." We somehow believe that we are superior to someone else by whatever measuring stick we choose to use. The error is that we usually use the wrong measuring stick.

To some who were confident of their own righteousness and looked down on everyone else, Jesus told this parable: "Two men went up to the temple to pray, one a Pharisee and the other a tax collector. The Pharisee stood by himself and prayed: 'God, I thank you that I am not like other people—robbers, evildoers, adulterers—or even like this tax collector. I fast twice a week and give a tenth of all I get.' "But the tax collector stood at a distance. He would not even look up to heaven, but beat his breast and said, 'God, have mercy on me, a sinner.' "I tell you that this man, rather than the other, went home justified before God. For all those who exalt themselves will be humbled, and those who humble themselves will be exalted" (Luke 18:9-14 NIV).

The Pharisee was confident in his own righteousness because he kept the law. He considered himself more deserving of God's love and blessings for that reason. He didn't realize that his heart was full of pride. As a Pharisee, he would have been well versed in the scriptures. Surely, he knew the proverb, "He mocks proud mockers but shows favor to the humble and oppressed" (Prov 3:34 NIV). Isaiah's prophecy, "The eyes of the arrogant will be humbled and human pride brought low; the Lord alone will be exalted in that day. The Lord Almighty has a day in store for all the proud and lofty, for all that is exalted (and they will be humbled)" (Isaiah 2:11-12 NIV) as well as the verse from Psalm 18: "You save the humble but bring low those whose eyes are haughty" (Ps. 18:27 NIV).

Rather than humbling himself before the Lord, the Pharisee compared himself to the tax collector. But he didn't use God's standard of measurement. God humbles the proud and exalts the humble. The tax collector acknowledged that he was a sinner. He confessed his sin and went away justified before God. The Pharisee did not. Self-exaltation is one symptom of the disease of pride that arises from comparing ourselves to others. It can keep us out of God's kingdom.

### FAVORITISM

We show favoritism when we choose to honor one person above another based on appearance or some other criteria.

> For if a man comes into your assembly with a gold ring and dressed in fine clothes, and there also comes in a poor man in dirty clothes, and you pay special attention to the one who is wearing the fine clothes, and say, "You sit here in a good place," and you say to the poor man, "You stand over there, or sit down by my footstool," have you not made distinctions among yourselves, and become judges with evil motives?" (James 2:2-4).

James addressed the issue of playing favorites based on appearance. The people thought the rich man had more to offer than the poor man, so they gave him greater honor and respect. James reminded them to obey the *royal law*, which is to love their neighbor as themselves. He meant, love each and every one the same as themselves, showing no partiality. If they showed favoritism, they were committing sin.

We do this all the time without even recognizing it. When I used to interview a potential new client, I would instantly evaluate them by their appearance before they spoke a word. If they presented themselves well, I would assume that they had money and that I might take their case. If they looked shabby, I judged that the meeting was a waste of my time. I compared their appearance to my standard of an acceptable client.

We've all had to attend networking mixers at some point in our lives. We always look for a safe person to talk to first. When we start to feel a little more comfortable, we look for the person who we think can benefit us the most and ignore the rest. That's only natural, of course, but what if we went into the mixer thinking about how we might help someone, rather than how they might help us? Comparing can cause us to play favorites.

### ENVY

Envy and jealousy are closely related. Envy is when we don't have something that someone else has. Jealousy is when someone threatens something we already have.

King David was the most powerful man alive. There was almost nothing he didn't have, but he wanted Bathsheba, the wife of Uriah. David compared what he had, the whole kingdom of Israel, to what he didn't have. Remember that Uriah is listed as one of David's mighty men (2 Samuel 23:39). It's probably safe to assume that Uriah was David's friend. Yet David committed adultery with Bathsheba and had Uriah killed to cover up his affair. David took Bathsheba into his house, but the child that she conceived died. Though he repented, David's sexual sin tainted his family forever. In the years that followed,

David's son Amnon raped David's daughter Tamar. In revenge, Absalom, another of David's sons, killed Amnon. Alienated from his father, Absalom eventually started a revolution against David. In retribution, David's general, Joab, killed Absalom. All was well in David's life until he started comparing what he had to what he didn't have.

Cain and Abel are another example of the fruits of envy. In Genesis 4, we read that Abel was a keeper of flocks, and Cain worked the ground. When it was time to sacrifice to the Lord, Cain brought an offering of the fruit of the ground. Abel offered the best of his flock. God approved of Abel's offering but had no regard for Cain's offering. God noticed that Cain was depressed because Abel received God's blessing, but Cain did not. God said to Cain, "Why are you angry? And why has your countenance fallen? If you do well, will not your countenance be lifted up? And if you do not do well, sin is crouching at the door, and its desire is for you, but you must master it" (Genesis 4:6-7). Although not explicitly stated in the text, it can be inferred from the context that God told Cain to present a sacrificial offering rather than just 'an offering of the fruit of the ground,' and he would have received the same blessing Abel received. Instead, Cain was so envious of God's approval of Abel, that he killed his own brother. Comparison leads us to envy, wanting what someone else has. Whether it's knowledge, a woman, or God's blessing, when we compare, we become envious, and envy can lead to murder.

## JEALOUSY

Remember, jealousy is when someone threatens to take what is already ours. In 1 Samuel 17, we read the story of David and Goliath. But before we look at that story, don't forget that Saul was king at the time. Saul was taller and more pleasing in appearance than all others. By comparison, he looked more like a king than anyone else. As king, and the most physically imposing, Saul should have been the one to fight Goliath, but he refused. David was just a young man, perhaps even a teenager at the time. But he volunteered to fight Goliath. David took five smooth stones from a brook, put one in his sling and flung it at Goliath. The stone penetrated Goliath's forehead and knocked him out cold. David quickly cut off Goliath's head and led a parade back into Israel. Saul was grateful that Goliath was dead, but he didn't anticipate how the people would love David for his heroics.

> And the women sang to one another as they celebrated, "Saul has struck down his thousands, and David his ten thousands." And Saul was very angry, and this saying displeased him. He said, "They have ascribed to David ten thousands, and to me they have ascribed thousands, and what more can he have but the kingdom?" And Saul eyed David from that day on (1 Sam. 18:7-9).

Saul compared himself to David because of the song that the women sang, and he became very jealous. He wanted to keep the kingdom. He wanted the people's respect and admiration. He jealously guarded these things. But after hearing the song the women sang, Saul knew the people favored David, and that David could eventually become king. He wanted to eliminate that threat, so Saul spent the next twenty years trying to kill David. David was not jealous for Saul's kingdom though. David had two chances to kill Saul but refused to kill the man God had made king. David was a fierce warrior, and he would have been a very useful asset to Saul if Saul had treated him well. Instead,

David was a fugitive from Saul. David was not there to fight alongside Saul in the battle that claimed Saul's life as recorded in 1 Kings 31. Had Saul not been jealous to protect his kingdom from David, he may have been able to save his kingdom, and his life.

## RACISM AND PREJUDICE

The Book of Genesis ends with Joseph's death and burial. Remember that after Joseph's brothers sold him into slavery, Joseph had miraculously risen to the position of second in command in Egypt next to Pharaoh. Joseph brought his father and 11 brothers to Egypt to live there during the famine. While in Egypt, the Israelites began to multiply. Joseph died, and several hundred years passed between the end of Genesis and the beginning of Exodus. The multitude of Israelites in Egypt threatened the Egyptians. They perceived that the Israelites were more numerous and mightier than they were. Comparing themselves along racial and religious lines, this is what happened next.

Now a new king arose over Egypt, who did not know Joseph. He said to his people, "Behold, the people of the sons of Israel are more and mightier than we. Come, let us deal wisely with them, or else they will multiply and in the event of war, they will also join themselves to those who hate us, and fight against us and depart from the land." So they appointed taskmasters over them to afflict them with hard labor. And they built for Pharaoh storage cities, Pithom and Raamses. But the more they afflicted them, the more they multiplied and the more they spread out, so that they were in dread of the sons of Israel. The Egyptians compelled the sons of Israel to labor rigorously; and they made their lives bitter with hard labor in mortar and bricks and at all kinds of labor in the field, all their labors which they rigorously imposed on them (Exodus 1:8-14).

It sounds a lot like the shameful tradition of American slavery, doesn't it? It's discrimination and oppression against a group of people that's either racially, ethnically, or religiously different. The Israelites were slaves in Egypt for 400 years before Moses led them out of Egypt. American slavery continued for over 200 years before our country abolished it. How despicable it is when we compare ourselves to others and then oppress them because they are different racially, ethnically, or religiously from us.

### INJUSTICE

On the night of Jesus' trial, Peter denied that he knew Jesus three times. The third time, Peter heard the rooster crow and remembered that Jesus had predicted that Peter would do this, and he wept bitterly. After Jesus' resurrection, He graciously restored Peter asking him three times if he loved Jesus and told Peter three times to take care of Jesus' sheep.

Then Jesus said to Peter: Truly, truly, I say to you, when you were younger, you used to gird yourself and walk wherever you wished; but when you grow old, you will stretch out your hands and someone else will gird you, and bring you where you do not wish to go." Now this He said, signifying by what kind of death he would glorify God. And when He had spoken this, He said to him, "Follow Me!" (John 21:18-19).

I DON'T KNOW IF PETER KNEW EXACTLY WHAT JESUS MEANT WHEN Jesus spoke those words. The first sentence of verse 19 is John's commentary on what Jesus said to Peter, written years later. It's hard to tell whether Peter understood that Jesus was referring to the death he would die, or whether John remembered Jesus' words to Peter after Peter's violent death. But Peter knew enough to be alarmed, and to ask what fate awaited John.

This is what happened next:

> Peter, turning around, saw the disciple whom Jesus loved following them; the one who also had leaned back on His bosom at the supper and said, "Lord, who is the one who betrays You?" So Peter seeing him said to Jesus, "Lord, and what about this man?" Jesus said to him, "If I want him to remain until I come, what is that to you? You follow Me!" (John 21:20-21)

Peter fell into the trap of comparing God's plan for his life with God's plan for John's life. God doesn't owe us a long life, or a peaceful death. Peter thought it was unjust that he would die a violent death at the hands of persecutors while, in his mind, John was getting off scot-free. Peter was wrong, of course. God calls us to different lives and to different deaths. The potter has the right to do what he wants with his clay. When we compare our suffering with the suffering of others, or when we compare our circumstances to anyone else's, we fall into the same trap as Peter.

### SHAME AND INSECURITY

Sarai, (whom God later renamed Sarah), was ashamed that she could not bear Abraham's children. Barrenness was a stigma in that society. But after they had been married for many years, God appeared to Abraham and promised him that he would be the father of many nations. How could that be when Sarah was barren? Sarah became impatient waiting for God to fulfill His promise. After all, God didn't specifically say that Abraham would be the father of many nations *through her*. So, Sarah cooked up a scheme to give her maid Hagar to Abraham so that she could bear his children. The child would still be considered Sarah's even though Hagar actually gave birth according to the custom of the time. The plan worked. Hagar conceived.

> "When she [Sarai] saw that she [Hagar] had conceived, her mistress was despised in her sight. And Sarai said to Abram, "May the wrong done me be upon you. I gave my maid into your arms, but when she saw that she had conceived, I was despised in her sight. May the Lord judge between you and me." But Abram said to Sarai, "Behold, your maid is in your power; do to her what is good in your sight." So Sarai treated her harshly, and she fled from her presence" (Gen. 16:4-6).

Sarah's impatience with God started the problem. But then Sarah couldn't help comparing herself, the barren wife, to Hagar, the fruitful maid. She couldn't stand the way Hagar walked around the house, lording it over Sarah even though Sarah was lord over her. So she made it so uncomfortable for Hagar that Hagar fled the home. Sarah compared up, from what she didn't have to what Hagar did have. Years later, when she gave birth to Isaac, she compared down from her position as wife of Abraham and mother of the child of the promise, to the lowly maid and her illegitimate son. In Genesis 21:10 she said to Abraham, "Drive out this maid and her son, for the son of this maid shall not be an heir with my son Isaac." How the tables had turned. First, Sarah's barrenness caused her shame; later, the presence of Hagar and Ishmael caused her insecurity.

I want to use a 21st century example of how comparison causes shame and insecurity. I want you to think about the evil of pornography. It destroys so many lives. I'm not even talking about how pornography exploits girls and women, and that sometimes filmmakers and traffickers threaten them with death if they don't perform. I'm talking now about the consumer. The reason why pornography is so destructive to people and to families is because of comparison. Men want their wives to look and act like the women on the screen. Men compare their wives to the fantasy presented to them, and they want what they see. Women can never live up to those unreasonable expectations. They may feel shame if they don't measure up, and insecurity that their husbands might discard them.

Another problem is that men compare themselves to the men in the movies. The average man does not look like the actor in the film, and he can't perform like him either. In the back of his mind, even though he wants his wife to be like the fantasy woman, he knows he can't be like the fantasy man. He thinks, "There are men out there who can please my wife better than I can." Pornography is a silent killer of marriages and souls. It causes shame, insecurity and sometimes anger. Most marriages cannot bear up under the weight of pornography addiction. Comparison is one of the forgotten culprits of why pornography is so destructive to marriages, families, and addicts alike.

## BIBLICAL COMPARISONS WE SHOULD MAKE

Comparing ourselves to others can cause many problems; however, the Bible also uses comparison positively. Let's look at when the Bible says it's right to compare.

### GOD'S PERFECT RIGHTEOUSNESS VS. OUR SINFUL NATURE

We should compare our own lack of righteousness with God's standard of righteousness, so that we can recognize how sinful we are and realize our need for a savior. "For all have sinned and fall short of the glory of God, being justified as a gift by His grace through the redemption which is in Christ Jesus" (Rom. 3:23-24). We can't get to heaven by judging ourselves good enough based on comparing our conduct with others. But that's what many people do. That kind of comparison is deadly because we are comparing ourselves to an imperfect standard. Comparing ourselves to Jesus' standard can lead to our salvation, because we will only rely on Jesus for salvation when we realize that only He is perfect.

### FALSE TEACHERS VS. TRUE TEACHERS

We must compare what false teachers say against what the Bible says, or they could lead us into heresy. Here are two of many scripture passages that warn about false teachers:

> But false prophets also arose among the people, just as there will also be false teachers among you, who will secretly introduce destructive heresies, even denying the Master who bought them, bringing swift destruction upon themselves. Many will follow their sensuality, and because of

them the way of the truth will be maligned; and in *their* greed, they will exploit you with false words; their judgment from long ago is not idle, and their destruction is not asleep (2 Pet. 2:1-3).

Dear friends, do not believe every spirit, but test the spirits to see whether they are from God, because many false prophets have gone out into the world. This is how you can recognize the Spirit of God: Every spirit that acknowledges that Jesus Christ has come in the flesh is from God, but every spirit that does not acknowledge Jesus is not from God. This is the spirit of the antichrist, which you have heard is coming and even now is already in the world (1 John 4:1-3 NIV).

We will only recognize false teachers if we compare what they say to what the Bible says. We are to be like the Bereans of Acts 17: "Now the Berean Jews were of more noble character than those in Thessalonica, for they received the message with great eagerness and examined the Scriptures every day to see if what Paul said was true" (Acts 17:11 NIV).

### OUR PRESENT SUFFERING VS. ETERNAL GLORY

If we didn't know that heaven awaited us, and all we knew were the sufferings in this life, we would become miserable people with no hope. Paul encouraged the Corinthian church. "For our light and momentary troubles are achieving for us an eternal glory that far outweighs them all. So we fix our eyes not on what is seen, but on what is unseen, since what is seen is temporary, but what is unseen is eternal" (2 Cor. 4:17-18). Paul had been through an unbelievable amount of hardship by the time he wrote this letter. Beatings, exposure, shipwreck, imprisonment, hunger, and yet he was able to keep his tribulations in proper perspective because he compared them to the eternal glory that awaited him. That's heaven. Eternal life with Jesus Christ. He recognized that his earthly life was just a short blip compared with eternal life, and so he was able to endure the hardship.

### SPIRITUAL VS. MATERIAL WEALTH

We should also compare and value spiritual wealth over material wealth. Jesus said in the Sermon on the Mount: "Do not store up for yourselves treasures on earth, where moths and vermin destroy, and where thieves break in and steal. But store up for yourselves treasures in heaven, where moths and vermin do not destroy, and where thieves do not break in and steal" (Matt. 6:19-20 NIV). Earthly treasure won't last. Spiritual treasure in heaven will last eternally. You can only spend a dollar once. Where will you invest your money? Compare and decide whether to invest in material or spiritual things.

### WHO YOU WERE BEFORE GOD SAVED YOU VS. WHO YOU ARE TODAY

Peter wrote in his first epistle, "Always be prepared to give an answer to everyone who asks you to give the reason for the hope that you have" (1 Pet. 3:15 NIV). In the vocabulary of our day, we might say, "Always be prepared to give your testimony." Your testimony is your story about who you were before Christ, what Christ did in your life to draw you to Himself, and what your life is like today as a result. Peter encouraged us to be prepared because others will notice a change in us. They may have compared the person they thought they knew with the person they see today and ask us what has changed. God may use us to bring someone else to salvation if we can answer them.

You will notice that in each of these examples where we *should* compare, the comparison is spiritual, not material or physical. Comparison is good when it shows us our need for a savior, when it helps us distinguish false from true teaching, when we must negotiate our way through the trials of life, when we are deciding where to invest our treasure, or when we are comparing our lives before and after Christ. These comparisons are Biblical and useful. The common thread of comparison that leads to terrible consequences is that they result from comparing ourselves physically and materially to others. We should not be in the game of comparing ourselves with others. We are all different. God has a different calling for each one of us. When we start to compare ourselves with others, the results are often disastrous. So, how can we get out of this rut?

## HOW TO GET OUT OF THE COMPARISON GAME

At the root of comparison is the desire to find our identity and worth in competing and comparing what we have with others. But our identity is not found in what we have, our identity is in who we are, or perhaps better said, *whose* we are. We can leave the comparison game behind by following a few simple suggestions.

### *Find your identity in Christ*

Many people find their identity in what they do or what they have. If we find our identity in our jobs and our possessions, we won't be able to resist comparing ourselves to others. For Christians, our jobs and portfolios are not who we are. Our sense of identity and purpose do not come from these things. We derive our identity and purpose from being believers in Jesus Christ, saved from the penalty of sin by His grace. If our goal is to please Him rather than to impress others, we can get out of the comparison game. We won't have to worry about what anyone else has or does. We won't be looking horizontally at others; we'll look vertically at Him.

Paul recognized who he was in Christ's eyes:

> For I am the least of the apostles and do not even deserve to be called an apostle, because I persecuted the church of God. But by the grace of God I am what I am, and his grace to me was not without effect. No, I worked harder than all of them—yet not I, but the grace of God that was with me (1 Cor. 15:9-10 NIV).

Paul almost fell into the trap of looking down on himself compared to the other apostles. Then he nearly looked down on the other apostles compared with how hard he worked. But he quickly caught himself and evaluated his ministry by his relationship to God. He thought, "it makes no difference how I see myself or how others see me. What matters is how Christ sees me."[1] If we could ever get that through our skulls, we could get out of the comparison game.

### REMEMBER THAT GOD MADE YOU UNIQUE

David said, "For you created my inmost being; you knit me together in my mother's womb. I praise you because I am fearfully and wonderfully made" (Ps. 139:13-14 NIV). Christians and pro-life advocates use these verses to prove that life begins at conception, and that's true. Abortion is a crime against God and the children He has created. But these verses also show that God doesn't make mistakes. He planned and determined everything about us before we were born. God is all-knowing and all-powerful. God created us just the way He wanted us to be. No two people are alike. Even identical twins are not the same. God loves variety. Just look around at the trees, flowers, and sky. He makes everything unique, including each of us, and He made us for a unique purpose. By grasping that God made us and loves us just the way we are, we can get out of the comparison game.

### BE GRATEFUL FOR WHAT YOU HAVE

When we are grateful for what we have, we won't pine for the things we don't have. We should be grateful that God gave us life. We should recognize that every gift that we have comes from Him (James 1:17). We should always remember that He has given us the gift of eternal life through the death and resurrection of His Son (Romans 5:8). If we spent our time being thankful for what we have, we wouldn't compare ourselves to others, or moan about the things that we don't have. God is eager to continue to bless people who are thankful for the blessings they already have.

### REMEMBER THAT THE BODY OF CHRIST NEEDS ALL OF US

In 1 Corinthians 12, Paul compared the different spiritual gifts that God has given us to the various parts of the body. The body won't function without each part doing its job. The same is true of the body of Christ. God has gifted each of us uniquely to fulfill a function in the body of Christ. We should know our spiritual gifts and use them for the glory of God, knowing that He gave us these gifts because He has work that He has prepared for us to do (Eph. 2:10). God has uniquely gifted us and prepared us for the work He has for us. We should be thankful for the gifts He has chosen to give us, rather than resentful of the ones He hasn't.


## CONCLUSION

All of this brings me back to where I began, my own journey with comparison. I never felt like I was a very good lawyer. It seemed that every lawyer I met was either smarter, more confrontational, more determined, or better prepared than I was. Maybe my heart was just never fully in it. My heart *is* fully in pastoring. There are always going to be larger churches, famous pastors, and preachers who sell millions of books, and sell out arenas on speaking tours. I have determined not to compare myself to them. God has a unique ministry planned for me that no one else can have. I am uniquely qualified to serve the people that God has given me to serve. I have no plans or ambitions to pastor some megachurch with thousands in attendance every Sunday. There's nothing wrong with that, it's just that I know myself well enough to know that I might not be able to handle the notoriety that comes with that.

Instead, God has entrusted me with a group of about 100 people who love the Lord, love His word, and strive to be more like Him every day. What a privilege it is to help to lead them where they already want to go! I'm grateful for the people that God has given me. I'm humbled that He took a sinful rebel like me, changed my heart, moved our family across the country, and gave me a ministry. It would be the height of arrogance to ask for anything else, unless it was for His glory and not mine. God has been faithful to me and my family. I'm satisfied in Him, and He is satisfied with me.

Gottfried Arnold wrote a beautiful hymn called "Bliss Beyond Compare" that sums up what we have in Christ compared to anything the world has to offer:

> Bliss beyond compare
> Which in Christ I share
> He's my only joy and treasure
> Tasteless is all worldly pleasure
> When in Christ I share[2]

# 9

## SICKNESS

**"This sickness will not end in death."**
**John 11:4**

In November 2018, Molly and I heard one of the scariest words in the English language: cancer. Molly went in for a routine mammogram, which revealed a suspicious lump. She had a biopsy, and a day or two later her doctor called just after she had arrived at work. He confirmed our worst fears. She came home and told me. We hugged each other, cried, and prayed. At that point, we didn't know what kind of breast cancer she had, how aggressive it was, the treatment options, or the prognosis. I'm sure we wouldn't have heard the words anyway. After you've heard the C word, it's hard to hear anything else.

The first day was one of the worst days of our lives. All you can feel is fear. On the second day, Molly regained her physical and spiritual strength and was ready to fight. It takes a day or two to find your footing after such shocking news. We had to remember that God allowed cancer, that God can heal it, and that God is in complete control. Those can be hard truths to swallow. Does God allow sickness? Why? If He plans to heal the sickness, why does He allow it in the first place? Why not just skip it? Why does God heal some illnesses and not others?

The Bible details many stories of people suffering various kinds of sickness and disease. Sometimes God allows it for reasons we may never know, like Job. Sometimes He allows it to discipline us for not living godly lives, like when God disciplined David for his sin with Bathsheba. Other times, He allows it so that He gets glory for the healing. An example is when Jesus healed the blind man in John 9. Sickness may just be the result of living in a fallen world caused by the sin of Adam and Eve in the Garden. How do we handle sickness when it intrudes on our lives? No one wants cancer, but God has a purpose in it. How we deal with it shows if we are trusting God in it and through it.

Before we begin, let's define sickness as I mean it in this chapter. Sickness comes in many forms. We've all had to suffer through the nuisance of a common cold. The runny nose, fever, sneezing, stuffy head, congested chest, and persistent cough are all very annoying. A cold may make us miserable for few days or weeks, but it passes. Most of us have had to deal with allergies that are particularly irritating at certain times of the year. Some people suffer with persistent headaches that Excedrin or Tylenol can remedy. God is sovereign over these minor illnesses too. But I'm talking in this chapter about chronic, painful, debilitating, even life-threatening disease or illness.

Sickness can be physical, mental, or emotional. Every one of us either has personally suffered, or knows someone who has had cancer, HIV/AIDS, Lou Gehrig's disease, Huntington's disease, cystic fibrosis, muscular dystrophy, multiple sclerosis, or some other debilitating disease. Then there are various of mental and emotional illnesses ranging from mild anxiety to depression, eating disorders, personality, and psychotic disorders. Again, the list could go on and on.

Doctors can cure some of these conditions and treat or manage others. The first thing that we must understand if we are going to be able to cope with sickness, is that God is sovereign over it. Nothing happens without it passing through God's hands first, and He can cure it whenever He wants.

## GOD'S SOVEREIGNTY OVER SICKNESS

God created a perfect world. Then He created Adam and Eve and placed them in the Garden of Eden, to tend the garden and to rule over His creation. When God finished creating, He said, "It is good." The only restriction He placed on them was that He did not allow them to eat from the tree of the knowledge of good and evil. He told them that on the day they ate of it, they would surely die. In Genesis 3, Eve fell victim to Satan's temptation to eat from the forbidden tree. She ate and shared with Adam. Although Adam and Eve eventually died, they didn't die immediately; however, all the conditions that cause sickness and death entered the world that day. That's called, *the Fall*.

The sickness and death that entered the world at the Fall still exist today. Unless Jesus returns first, we will all die because sin ~nd death entered the world when Adam and Eve sinned. While ~ve live in the knowledge that God is sovereign over ~ world, including sickness and death. He ~he Bible. Not only is God sovereign also use sickness to achieve His own

### GOD ALLOWS SICKNESS TO WIN VICTORY OVER SATAN – JOB

Job's story is unique in all of Scripture. It's only in his life that we see that there is an unceasing cosmic battle raging in the spiritual realm between God and Satan, and the forces of good and evil. God can end this battle any second that He wants to, but for reasons known only to Him, He has allowed Satan some dominion over the world for a limited time. In Job, God offers us a glimpse behind the curtain. The reader understands that Job is in the middle of this cosmic battle. Job never finds out.

As the book begins, Satan enters God's presence and God says to him:

> "Have you considered my servant Job? For there is no one like him on the earth, a blameless and upright man, fearing God and turning away from evil." Then Satan answered the Lord, "Does Job fear God for nothing? Have You not made a hedge about him and his house and all that he has, on every side? You have blessed the work of his hands, and his possessions have increased in the land. But put forth Your hand now and touch all that he has; he will surely curse You to Your face" (Job 1:8-11).

God allowed Satan to take everything that Job had, but not to touch Job. Satan used invading armies and hostile weather to demolish his home, kill his children, and destroy his livestock. When Job did not curse God, Satan challenged God further, saying, "All that a man has he will give for his life. However, put forth Your hand now, and touch his bone and his flesh; he wi[ll] curse You to Your face." (Job 2:4-5). God allowed Satan to af[flict] Job, but not to kill Him. Satan caused sores over every i[nch of] Job's body that made him so miserable that he wanted t[o]

. . .

JOB DID NOT CURSE GOD; HOWEVER, HE DID DEMAND AN audience with Him. Over the next thirty-six chapters, Job insisted to his friends that he had committed no sin deserving punishment, and he pleaded for the chance to vindicate himself before God. At the end of the book, God finally entered the drama. He cross-examined Job, challenging his right to demand answers from God, saying, "Who is this that darkens counsel by words without knowledge? Where were you when I laid the foundations of the earth" (Job 38:2, 4a).

God silenced Job. Job repented of his pride in thinking that he had a right to question God. Afterward, God restored Job's health and his fortune, and gave him another family. But Job never got his first family back. God is sovereign. He allows sickness, disease, and even death. Job had done nothing to deserve the catastrophe, but God has the right to do what He wants for His own purposes. We who read Job understand that God allowed it so that we would know that God wins all cosmic battles. God triumphs over Satan, and good triumphs over evil. But Job never discovered God's purposes. Likewise, we may never know why God allows sickness, disease, and death, in our lives, but we still must trust that He is sovereign, and that He is good.

## DISCIPLINES WITH SICKNESS

...mands proper worship and honor. There are many ...of God using sickness to discipline people ...nor God properly.

...etails most of the events of Uzziah's life.

He rose to the throne of Judah when he was only sixteen years old. He enjoyed a long and successful reign in the middle of the 8th Century BC. During his fifty-two years on the throne, he defeated the Philistines repeatedly. The Ammonites paid him tribute. Uzziah built towers in Jerusalem and in the wilderness. He dug many cisterns to water his livestock. He had an army ready to defeat any who would challenge Judah. His fame spread everywhere. By any measure, Uzziah was a very successful king. But it all went to his head. Pride was his undoing. Verse sixteen tells us, "But when he became strong, his heart was so proud that he acted corruptly, and he was unfaithful to the Lord his God, for he entered the temple of the Lord to burn incense on the altar of incense" (2 Chron. 26:16).

Uzziah was a powerful king, but not a priest. God appointed only the priests to burn incense in the temple. The other priests tried to talk Uzziah out of it, but they could not dissuade him. Instead he raged against the priests who tried to stop him. He burnt the incense, and immediately, leprosy broke out on his forehead. The priests rushed him out of the temple, but God had already judged Uzziah. God's law required isolation of lepers from the people. Uzziah was now unclean with leprosy. God left him in leprous solitude until the day of his death, cursed with sickness and disease as discipline for his disobedience.

### HEROD AGRIPPA I

Acts 12 recounts the story of King Herod Agrippa's mu[...] of James the apostle, and his attempted murder of Pete[...] supernaturally escaped the sword with the help of [...] After Peter's escape, Herod went home to Caesarea t[...]

political conflict with the people of Tyre and Sidon. Herod was angry with them for some unreported reason. Because the two cities were dependent on Herod for food, they needed to appease him. They won the approval of Herod's chamberlain, who granted them an audience with the king.

Herod clothed himself in his best royal apparel for the occasion and sat on his judgment seat to wait for his enemies to heap praises on him. As Herod spoke, verse 22 says, "The people kept crying out, 'The voice of a god and not of a man.'" God disciplined Herod for receiving worship: "And immediately an angel of the Lord struck him because he did not give God the glory, and he was eaten by worms and died" (Acts 12:23). That sounds like a particularly gruesome death. The Jewish historian Josephus says that it took *five days* for him to die.[1] God disciplined him with sickness, disease, and death for accepting the praise as though he were God, and not giving glory to the One True God.

### DAVID'S CHILD WITH BATHSHEBA

One of God's punishments on David for his sin with Bathsheba was the death of the child of his sin. "The Lord also has taken away your sin; you shall not die. However, because by this deed you have given occasion to the enemies of the Lord to ˋˋᵇheme, the child also that is born to you shall surely die" (2 ᵔ ᵔ14). The child became very sick and died seven days ᵐ that justice would require that God cause ˋᵗ God's discipline was worse. I can't ᵢ child. I'd much rather die myself. his sin. It was not only the physical ₒn, but the emotional pain of knowing ₒn's death, and Bathsheba's grief.

. . .

### NADAB AND ABIHU

In Leviticus 10, we read of Aaron's two sons Nadab and Abihu. "Now Nadab and Abihu, the sons of Aaron, took their respective firepans, and after putting fire in them, placed incense on it and offered strange fire before the Lord, which He had not commanded them And fire came out from the presence of the Lord and consumed them, and they died before the Lord" (Lev. 10:1-2). Most scholars agree that either Nadab and Abihu were drunk, or that they offered fire from their own firepans, rather than fire from the altar.[2] God disciplined them with death for not worshiping Him properly.

### UZZAH

God gave rules for how to transport the ark of the covenant in Numbers 4. God charged the Kohathites (a division of the Levites) with the responsibility for transporting the ark using poles inserted through the rings on the ark. 1 Chronicles 13 tells us that David was bringing the ark from Kiriath-Jearim to Jerusalem, but he was not following the instructions God had given. David transported the ark on a cart pulled by oxen, rather than having the Kohathites carry it. The oxen somehow upset the ark as they were pulling it. A man named Uzzah reached out to save the ark from falling off the cart. Without proper background, we might think that God was too harsh with Uzzah. But the ark should not have been on the cart in the fir place, and Uzzah, a non-Kohathite, should not have anywhere near it. Though his intentions may have been God disciplined him with death for his transgression.

. . .

*THE CORINTHIAN BELIEVERS*

In his letter to the Corinthians, Paul gave instructions about how the people could eat the Lord's Supper. He said,

> Therefore whoever eats the bread or drinks the cup of the Lord in an unworthy manner, shall be guilty of the body and the blood of the Lord. But a man must examine himself, and in so doing he is to eat of the bread and drink of the cup. For he who eats and drinks, eats and drinks judgment to himself if he does not judge the body rightly. For this reason many among you are weak and sick, and a number sleep (1 Cor 11:27-30).

Sleep is a euphemism for death. Sickness and death were God's discipline on certain members of the Corinthian church for failure to take the Lord's Supper with the proper attitude of worship. God is sovereign over disease and can use it to discipline his people. However, he also can receive glory through healing sickness.

## GOD ALLOWS SICKNESS TO RECEIVE GLORY THROUGH HEALING

Sometimes God allows sickness just so He can heal it. Healing is a demonstration of God's power and sovereignty over sickness. When God heals, He receives glory.

pel, Jesus and his disciples passed a who had been blind from birth. His who sinned, this man or his parents, born blind?' Jesus answered, 'It *was* neither *that* this man sinned, nor his parents; but it was so that the works of God might be displayed in him'" (John 9:2-3). Jesus then spit on the ground to make a mud salve that he spread on the eyes of the blind man, and immediately, he could see. This prompted a debate between the blind man and the Pharisees about Jesus' identity. The blind man said he was a prophet. The Pharisees said he was a sinner. The blind man corrected the Pharisees by telling them that God does not answer the prayers of sinners, but only the God-fearing and those who do His will. The Pharisees didn't like being lectured by this man whom they considered to be far beneath them, so they put him out of the synagogue.

It was then that Jesus found the man a second time and said to him, "'Do you believe in the Son of Man?' He answered, 'Who is He, Lord, that I may believe in Him?' Jesus said to him, 'You have both seen Him, and He is the one who is talking with you.' And he said, 'Lord, I believe.' And he worshiped Him" (John 9:36-38). Jesus healed the man so He could save him from his sins, and so that God could get the glory.

*LAZARUS*

In John 11, we read:

Now a certain man was sick, Lazarus of Bethany, the village of Mary and her sister Martha. It was the Mary who anointed the Lord with ointment, and wiped His feet with her hair, whose brother Lazarus was sick. So the sisters sent word to Him, saying, "Lord, behold, he whom You love is sick." But when Jesus heard this, He said, "This sickness is not to end in death, but for the glory of God, so that the Son of God may be glorified by it." Now Jesus loved Martha and her sister and

Lazarus. So when He heard that he was sick, He then stayed two days longer in the place where He was (John 11:1-6).

Doesn't Jesus' response seem strange? He heard that Lazarus was sick so He stayed in the place where he was two days longer? At the end of John 10, Jesus was in Bethany beyond the Jordan, the place where John was first baptizing, a different Bethany than the one near Jerusalem. It was about twenty miles from where Lazarus was, a full-day's walk. The Jews believed that the soul hovered over the body for about four days before it left. Death was not considered *permanent* according to the superstition, until after the fourth day. Lazarus probably died the same day that the messenger left Bethany beyond the Jordan to return to Mary and Martha. It would have taken a day for the messenger to reach Jesus with the news of Lazarus' sickness. After waiting two more days, followed by a day-long walk to Bethany on the fourth day, according to the superstition, Lazarus' soul would be gone. No one would have doubted whether he was truly dead. Because Jesus waited, God could be fully glorified.

When Jesus arrived, Lazarus' sister Martha met Jesus and said,

"Lord, if You had been here, my brother would not have died. Even now I know that whatever You ask of God, God will give You." Jesus said to her, "Your brother will rise again." Martha said to Him, "I know that he will rise again in the resurrection on the last day." Jesus said to her, "I am the resurrection and the life; he who believes in Me will live even if he dies, and everyone who lives and believes in Me will never die. Do you believe this?" (John 11:21-26).

Jesus faced a similar reproach from Martha's sister, Mary, in verse 32. Jesus asked them to show Him where they had buried Lazarus. When he arrived at the tomb,

> Jesus raised His eyes, and said, "Father, I thank You that You have heard Me. I knew that You always hear Me; but because of the people standing around I said it, so that they may believe that You sent Me." When He had said these things, He cried out with a loud voice, "Lazarus, come forth." The man who had died came forth, bound hand and foot with wrappings, and his face was wrapped around with a cloth. Jesus said to them, "Unbind him, and let him go." Therefore many of the Jews who came to Mary, and saw what He had done, believed in Him (John 11:41-45).

God used Lazarus' sickness and death to receive glory. Before Jesus called Lazarus from the tomb, He prayed to God, not for His own benefit, but for the witnesses who were about to see the miracle. The miracle was proof that Jesus was who He claimed to be. God received glory because Jesus asked God for the miracle first. God received even more glory because the Jews who saw the miracle believed that God sent Jesus. Jesus' fame continued to grow, and the crowds grew larger.

In the next chapter, we read that "the large crowd of the Jews then learned that He was there (in Bethany); and they came, not for Jesus' sake only, but that they might also see Lazarus, whom He raised from the dead" (John 12:9.) "The Jews" refers to the Jewish leadership. They came looking for Jesus and Lazarus with evil intent, as we read in verse 10: "But the chief priests planned to put Lazarus to death also." But the miracle that Jesus performed continued to bear fruit for the glory of God. The Jews' motive was to kill Jesus and Lazarus, "because on account of him many of the Jews were going away *and were believing in Jesus* (John 12:11).

Probably, the massive crowds that were present at Jesus' triumphal entry can also be attributed to raising Lazarus. It's impossible to say how many converts Jesus made in Jerusalem that can be traced back to Jesus' raising of Lazarus from the dead, and God received glory through all of it.

Jesus did many other healing miracles to convince the people that He was the Messiah that He claimed to be. When Jesus came down the mountain after delivering the Sermon on the Mount, He performed nine miracles of healing. He healed a leper, the centurion's servant, Peter's mother in law, a demoniac, a paralytic, Jairus' daughter, a woman who had been bleeding for twelve years, a blind man, and a mute man. I could go on and on citing Jesus' miracles of healing. A common thread throughout them is that God allowed sickness so that Jesus could prove that He had the authority that He claimed to have. When people saw Jesus' miracles and believed, God received glory.

Why does God seek glory? Is He an egomaniac? Did he take everything Job had, including his health and his family, just to make a point with Satan? Did he punish all these people with death and disease just because they didn't worship Him the way He wanted? Did he afflict others with disease only so he could heal them and receive glory for it? Does God need us to stroke His massive ego so that He won't curse us with sickness and death? Not at all!

I like the way John Piper answered the question. He writes:

> God is most glorified in us when we are most satisfied in him, because the answer to the question of whether God is an egomaniac or not is whether his self-exaltation is at the same

time a satisfaction of our souls. And that is, in fact, what the Bible says. The reason God in exalting himself is not an egomaniac, is because he is exalting the very thing that satisfies my soul, namely his beauty, his glory, his character.[3]

God uses all things to point us to Himself because He is the answer to all our troubles and problems. Psalm 119:91 says, "All things are Your servants." All things include sickness, suffering, disease, and death. If that's not a satisfying answer, then consider this. God loves us so much that He caused His own Son to suffer more than sickness. He caused Him to suffer death, not as discipline for His own sins, but for ours. The sinless Son of God, who lived a perfect life on earth, suffered the worst discipline imaginable at the hands of sinners, death on a Roman cross. Not without God's knowledge, or against His will, but according to His *plan*! It had to be that way for God to save us. God had to do for us what we could not do for ourselves. We have all sinned and fallen short of God's glory (Romans 3:23). We can't get to heaven in our sinful state.

The only way for God to remove the stain of our sin was to take our punishment for it Himself. He bore our sins on the cross and died for them. When we believe in Him for our salvation, God wipes our slate full of sins clean. He forgives us.

As I write, the world is in the grip of Covid-19. We don't know why God is allowing it, but we do know that God has a purpose in it. We pray for God's mercy and that He will use it to cause a worldwide revival. We pray that through this and all sickness, God will cause us to see His glory and Jesus' love displayed on the cross and lead us to repent of our sins and trust in Him for our salvation. If God must use sickness, disease and even death to draw us to Himself, He will. And it's a small price to pay. Our eternity is at stake.

## HOW SHOULD WE RESPOND TO SICKNESS?

None of us wants to be sick. Our usual response is to whine and complain about it, and pray that it passes quickly. What if we tried a new approach? What if we sought God's purposes in it? How can we do that?

### BY EXAMINING OUR LIVES FOR SIN

The book of Hebrews explains that God disciplines us for our own good.

> But if you are without discipline, of which all have become partakers, then you are illegitimate children and not sons. Furthermore, we had earthly fathers to discipline us, and we respected them; shall we not much rather be subject to the Father of spirits, and live? For they disciplined us for a short time as seemed best to them, but He disciplines us for our good, so that we may share His holiness. All discipline for the moment seems not to be joyful, but sorrowful; yet to those who have been trained by it, afterwards it yields the peaceful fruit of righteousness (Hebrews 12:8-11).

If we are ill, it may be that it's because there is sin or disobedience in our lives. Other times, sickness comes from lifestyle choices that we make. We eat too much and are overweight, which leads to high blood pressure and cholesterol or diabetes. Alcohol abuse and smoking are killers. Bad sexual choices, even one, can lead to all kinds of disease, suffering, and even death. Examine your life. Is there anything that you need to repent of? If so, repent of it. If that's the reason you are sick, God will heal it. The sickness will have achieved its purpose.

But if sin is not prevalent in our lives, God may have some other reason for our illness, just like He had for Job's, and we may never know the reason

### BY RECOGNIZING THAT SICKNESS IS PART OF THE FALLEN WORLD

The fact that we live in a fallen, sinful world may also be the reason for our sickness.

> For the creation was subjected to futility, not willingly, but because of Him who subjected it, in hope that the creation itself also will be set free from its slavery to corruption into the freedom of the glory of the children of God. For we know that the whole creation groans and suffers the pains of childbirth together until now. And not only this, but also we ourselves, having the first fruits of the Spirit, even we ourselves groan within ourselves, waiting eagerly for *our* adoption as sons, the redemption of our body (Romans 8:20-23).

Because of sin, corruption enslaves the world. The corruption isn't moral. It means physical deterioration or corrosion. The earth will deteriorate over time because of the weight and curse of sin. Our bodies too will wear out, they become sick and diseased, and they eventually die. It may not be our own sin that has caused our sickness, but the result of living in a sinful and fallen world. The world is accursed, and us with it. But God's promise is that Jesus is coming again to redeem our bodies and the world with them.

### BY SEEKING GOD'S PURPOSES INSTEAD OF COMPLAINING

Disease may interfere with our lives, but it doesn't have to own us. It may be our companion for a while, but we don't have to invite it to sit at the head of the table. God always has a purpose in sickness. Instead of spending our energy complaining about our illness, why not seek the lessons that God has for us in it? Paul wrote to the Roman Christians, "And we know that God causes all things to work together for good to those who love God, to those who are called according to His purpose" (Rom. 8:28). Can we identify any good things that have happened because of our sickness?

I have heard stories about people praying in hospitals for themselves or someone they love, and hospital staff comes to know the Lord through those prayers. I know sick people who have witnessed to everyone they know about how gracious and merciful God has been through their sickness. This spirit of optimism attracts people. They may want to know where it comes from, and they may come to faith in the Lord through our attitude toward illness. God might use our sickness to heal division within a family. The possibilities are endless. The point is that complaining is a waste of time and is quite unattractive, while glorifying God in our circumstances is incredibly attractive. If we have the right attitude about sickness, God can use it for His good purposes.

### By Glorifying God in healing

While Jesus was on His way to Jerusalem for His passion week, He entered a village where ten lepers were crying out, "Jesus, Master, have mercy on us." Jesus told them to go and show themselves to the priests. While they were on the way, they were each cleansed of their leprosy. Of the ten, only one of them turned back to Jesus to give thanks. "Now one of them, when he saw that he had been healed, turned back, glorifying

God with a loud voice, and he fell on his face at His feet, giving thanks to Him" (Luke 17:15-16). As soon as the other nine were cleansed, they immediately forgot who cleansed them and continued on their way. The one returned, gave God all the glory, and thanked and praised Jesus for His healing.

Let's remember that God heals us from sickness. Doctors and medicine are His tools for healing. God has given the gifts of science, medicine, and the body's own healing power to cure sickness and disease. Remember that God is the ultimate cause of all healing. Thank your doctor for his or her skill in helping you get well. But remember to praise God too. Healing would be impossible if God had not allowed doctors to diagnose the cause of the illness and use the tools of healing at their disposal.

## CONCLUSION

Molly's cancer diagnosis came on November 9, 2018. We spent the next several days visiting the surgeon and the oncologist to discuss treatment options and prognosis. Thankfully, they found it early. It was invasive lobular carcinoma, stage one. As far as they could tell from the sonograms, the tumor was about a half-centimeter in size and hadn't metastasized. The treatment options presented were to remove the tumor only, or to have either a single or double mastectomy. After considering the statistics predicting recovery and recurrence for each surgery and weighing the relative difficulty of the surgeries and recovery, we opted for removal of the tumor only. She had surgery on November 26, 2018.

Because of the kind of cancer, she was able to avoid chemotherapy. They treated her with radiation by catheter. After they removed the tumor, she had to have a second procedure to insert a catheter into the cavity that the tumor created. It looked like a fountain pen with a bunch of wires sticking out of it. With the catheter in place, she could go to the radiology doctor to begin treatments. Walking into a radiation facility for the first time was like walking into a new world that we didn't know existed. Patients filled the room, all people either waiting for cancer treatment, or waiting with a loved one.

When it was Molly's turn, the doctor connected the wires sticking out of her to a machine that sent radioactive seeds directly into the cavity and back out again. She had to do that twice a day for a week, compared to regular radiation which would have been once a day every day for 6 weeks. She had the radiation the week of December 10-14. Mind you, this was all during Thanksgiving and Christmas.

After Molly completed the radiation treatment, she visited with the surgeon, the oncologist, the radiation doctor, and other doctors for the next two weeks. She had a bone density scan and many other tests done. We were in a hurry not only to put cancer behind us, but also to finish treatment before the end of the year. If treatment extended into the new year, we would have to pay another huge deductible. Her last test was on December 27, the last day of the year that any doctor's office would be open.

As I look back, we had about forty doctor appointments from November 9 to December 27. Every door that we needed to open, miraculously opened for us just at the right time. As soon as we were ready for the next appointment, or to see the next specialist, an appointment was available. The surgery, the catheter, the radiation, the follow up, fell into place one right after another until Molly received a clean bill of health by year-end. She follows up with each doctor regularly and takes medicine daily to prevent recurrence. It wasn't easy, and there are difficult side effects from the medicine that she will have to take for five years, but the side effects are better than cancer.

As of today, there's no evidence of cancer in her. Praise be to God! I know that her cancer was not the result of God's discipline. Maybe it was so that we could tell this story, give glory to God and have other people come to know Him as a result. While Molly was in the waiting room for one of her radiation appointments, she met a woman who was broken-hearted dealing with her mother's cancer. Molly hugged her and prayed for her. God showed Molly that on that day, *that woman* was the reason why Molly was there. She has also had many opportunities to encourage other women with breast cancer in person, and also on a Facebook breast cancer support group page. Who knows how God will use Molly's cancer in the days and years to come? As I've said, the secret things belong to God. Just because she is cancer-free doesn't mean we can't use the experience to praise and glorify God.

I also know that many others don't have the same happy ending to their story. I can't explain that either. God is sovereign. He wants us to trust him. If Molly's cancer had been more serious, if she had required chemo, had her hair fall out, and suffer sickness for years, I pray that we would have glorified God through it all. We can only walk the path God gives us. We live knowing that it could come back or show up somewhere else. This is our path.

We know that unless the Lord returns first, we will all have to suffer through sickness and ultimately, death. The great news that we have is the same news that Jesus reported when He heard that Lazarus was sick, "This sickness will not end in death." Lazarus rose from the dead. Jesus raised him from the dead to show that He can raise us from the dead too. Though we will die physically, because of our faith in Jesus, our physical death is only a door to eternal spiritual life in heaven with Him. Our sickness does not end in death, it leads to life!

The last stanza of the hymn, "Rock of Ages", by Augustus Toplady expresses this hope that we have:

> While I draw this fleeting breath,
> When my eyelids close in death,
> When I soar to worlds unknown,
> See thee on thy judgment throne,
> Rock of Ages, shelter me!
> Let me hide myself in thee![4]

# 10

# COMPROMISE

**"Do not love the world or the things
in the world." 1 John 2:15**

I wrote about anxiety in Chapter 1. I mentioned at the end of that chapter that during my period of anxiety, I received very few job interviews, and how God used that for good. I did have a couple of interviews though, and during that process I learned a lot about compromise. In January 2015, I applied for several pastoral positions. We wanted to stay in Texas, but we knew that we should follow God's will wherever He led.

Two churches asked me to complete their application and questionnaire. One was for a senior pastor role at a church in New Jersey, about an hour from our former hometown. The other was for an associate pastor position at a church that was about fifteen minutes from our new home in Texas. After going through many months without an interview, to have two opportunities simultaneously seemed too good to be true.

.  .  .

THE JOB OF THE MEMBERS OF A PASTORAL SEARCH COMMITTEE IS challenging. Their responsibility is to decide what qualifications and experience their candidate must have. They write their advertisement and decide where to post it. They cull through sometimes hundreds of resumes, narrow the search down to about five, and schedule interviews. They invite the chosen candidates to preach and receive feedback from the congregation. Ideally, they bathe the entire process in prayer. When they finally call their pastor, they pray they have chosen the right candidate. Their work begins long before they ever contact the candidate, in this case, me. If the search committee chooses well, the church forgets who was on it. If they choose poorly, the congregation has a long memory!

My experience with the two search committees was very different. My first interview with the Texas church was with the senior pastor and his wife. Our courtship had a more business-like tenor than the New Jersey church, which had more of a personal feel.

After several interviews with the Texas church, several meet and greets with the members of the congregation, and preaching at the church three times, they offered me the associate pastor position. The salary they offered was less than what we needed to survive, so there would have to be some negotiation. There was another problem, though. I had committed to preach in the New Jersey church that coming Sunday. They had already paid for my family to fly and rent a car and were expecting me in five days. To bail out on them at that point would have meant leaving them without a preacher on Sunday, breaking my word to them, and wasting a lot of their money.

I expected the Texas church to understand the delicate position I was in, but they did not. They told me that if I went to

New Jersey to preach that Sunday, they would rescind their offer. That stunned me. I had no guarantee that the New Jersey church would offer me the position, or if I even wanted it. If I went, I would be throwing away the bird in the hand for the bird in the bush. But if I didn't go, I would compromise what I knew was right to secure the position in TX that I thought I wanted. What to do?

## COMPROMISE DEFINED

Miriam-Webster defines *compromise* as "the settlement of differences by arbitration or by consent reached by mutual concessions."[1] That's a correct definition when two or more parties are in dispute with each other. That's not the kind of compromise that I am talking about in this chapter. I'm talking about compromise with ourselves. We have standards of belief that we hold to be true, and standards of conduct and morality that we live by. We typically act in conformance with those standards. However, when the standards we hold come into conflict with something that we want, we can find ourselves tempted to set aside—compromise—those standards. In my story, if I wanted the associate pastor role that the Texas church offered, I had to leave the New Jersey church in the lurch, which was something I knew to be wrong.

We're faced with opportunities to compromise our beliefs and behaviors daily. What if you want a promotion at work, but you know that to get it, you need to help the company hide income so that it can avoid taxes? You know that what they are asking you to do is wrong, but you sure would like that promotion. It comes with a nice raise, more responsibility, and a bigger office and expense account. Are you willing to compromise your beliefs and break a few rules for the promotion? *That's an example of moral compromise.*

What if you're a Christian, and you really like the woman you just started dating, but you find out that she's not really a Christian? She believes in God abstractly but isn't interested in knowing Jesus as her personal savior and doesn't believe that He is the only way to heaven. She doesn't give religion a whole lot of thought, but she's okay with you believing. You take Christianity seriously. Are you willing to date, or even marry, an unbeliever? *That's an example of doctrinal compromise.*

## YIELDING TO COMPROMISE

The Bible has many examples of people faced with the opportunity to compromise either morally or doctrinally. Let's look at a few of these and see how damaging it can be.

### Reuben

Reuben was the oldest of Jacob's sons. He and his brothers hated their brother Joseph because their father Jacob loved him most. Joseph contributed to their animosity by insisting on telling his older brothers a dream he had where their sheaves of corn bowed down to his, and another one where the sun, moon and eleven stars were bowing down to him (Gen. 37:1-11).

Jacob sent Joseph's ten older brothers away to pasture a flock in Shechem. After some time, Jacob sent Joseph to check on them. He caught up with them further away at Dothan. His brothers saw him coming and plotted to kill him. Reuben was the only one who objected. His proposed compromise was to not shed Joseph's blood, but to throw him into a cistern instead. Reuben thought that if he could save Joseph's life then, he could return to rescue him later (v. 18-22). But circumstances got out of Reuben's control. After they put Joseph in the cistern, Reuben left the brothers for a brief time. During that time, the other brothers saw a band of Midianites coming and decided to pull Joseph from the cistern and sell him as a slave to the Midianites (v. 23-28).

Reuben returned later to find the cistern empty (v. 29-30). Joseph was gone! Reuben's plan failed. Unforeseen circumstances turned his moral compromise into catastrophe. With no other options available, Reuben and his brothers concocted a scheme to tell their father that wild beasts had killed Joseph. Joseph meanwhile went on to become second in command in Egypt and saved the world from famine. But the brothers couldn't have known that God would turn their evil into good. They had deprived Jacob of his favorite son and grieved him.

Whenever we lower our standards, there is always something behind the compromise that motivates it. Usually, we bend our standards for the sake of our comfort in one form or another. What motivated Reuben's compromise? He chose to do what was wrong to avoid conflict with his brothers. Reuben was trying to be a people pleaser. It was more comfortable for him to avoid conflict by waiting to rescue Joseph later. If anyone should have protected his younger brother Joseph, it should have been Reuben. As the oldest brother, he should have led by example. He should have demanded that the younger brothers not harm Joseph, and personally escorted Joseph home safely.

We often enter compromise with the hope of being able to correct it later. In the example of compromising to get the promotion, we might justify it by promising to correct corporate policy later, when we have more power and influence. But unforeseen events can prevent us from fixing things.

Reuben hoped to correct things later, but once the other brothers sold Joseph, the matter was out of his hands. Reuben couldn't do anything except to join the conspiracy to lie to their father. That's why it's so important to never compromise our morality. One sin leads to another. One lie begets another as we try to cover up the first lie with a second one. Conflict within families is nothing new. Joseph lived some 3700 years ago. Family conflict began when Adam blamed Eve for eating the forbidden fruit. Families will always have clashes. Are we willing to speak the truth and stand up for what is right? Or will we compromise our morals to avoid quarrels.


## SOLOMON

Solomon's story is among the most perplexing in the entire Bible. He was the wisest and richest king ever, but it wasn't enough for him. We learn in 1 Kings 11:1-3 that Solomon had 700 wives and 300 concubines. (I don't know how that's even possible, but that's a topic for another day!) God told Solomon not to marry foreign, pagan wives because they would lead him away from God and toward idol worship. Solomon was the wisest man on earth. He prayed for the wisdom he needed to rule the multitude, and God granted it to him. Surely, he knew that God's way was right. Still, Solomon compromised his beliefs and morals for his own personal comfort and pleasure.

We have a saying in our house: Partial obedience equals disobedience. In other words, you either obey fully or you are disobeying. Solomon didn't obey God fully, which meant that he was disobedient to Him. 1 Kings 11:4 says that Solomon's wives turned his heart from the Lord. He built altars for his other wives and drifted into paganism and idol worship (v. 7-8). He lowered his morals for physical pleasure and the results were catastrophic. As king of Israel, his subjects followed his example. Solomon led his nation away from God and into idolatry.

Before he died, Solomon wrote the book of Ecclesiastes, reflecting on the fact that he had tried every pleasure under the sun, and none of it satisfied him. In the end, he realized that only God could satisfy his longings. But he had lost sight of that when he was making compromises years earlier, trading purity for paganism, idol worship and sexual pleasure. After his death, civil war divided Israel into the northern kingdom of Israel and the southern kingdom of Judah. Both nations continued to practice idolatry until God finally punished them for it. Assyria exiled the northern kingdom in 722 BC, and Babylon exiled the southern kingdom in 586 BC. Compromise can have long-term and devastating results.

### PILATE

Pontius Pilate was the governor of Judea from 26-36 AD. He ruled over Jerusalem during Jesus' crucifixion and resurrection. Politics is a messy business as we all know. It wasn't any easier to be a politician in Pilate's day. The Jews hated him because he represented Rome. Pilate had also given the Jews real reasons to hate him. He killed Jews and mixed their blood with the blood of animal sacrifices. He stole from their temple treasury to build a Roman aqueduct. He installed images on the Jewish temple, which nearly caused a riot. In fact, the Jews wrote to Emperor Tiberias to complain about Pilate. Tiberias was Pilate's boss, and he rebuked Pilate harshly for doing things that would instigate the Jews and disturb the peace. Rome didn't want riots.

They wanted their governor to keep the peace. Pilate was in a precarious position with Emperor Tiberias when He was deciding what to do with Jesus. The table was set for compromise.

The Jews came to Pilate demanding that he sentence Jesus to crucifixion. They said that Jesus was a troublemaker and a blasphemer. Pilate believed that Jesus was innocent. He knew the Jews wanted to kill Jesus because they were envious of Him (Matt. 27:18). Pilate tried to avoid involvement by sending Jesus to Herod Antipas. When that didn't work, he tried to set Jesus free by having Him scourged instead, hoping that would satisfy the Jews. Next he attempted to release Jesus in keeping with the tradition that the governor would release one Jewish prisoner at Passover. Instead of asking for Pilate to release Jesus, the Jews asked for Barabbas. Pilate agonized over what to do with Jesus. His own wife told him "not to have anything to do with that righteous man," because she had suffered greatly in a dream about Jesus the night before (Matt. 27:19). But as Pilate was trying to avoid crucifying Jesus, the Jews cried out, "If you release this Man, you are no friend of Caesar; everyone who makes himself out to be a king opposes Caesar" (John 19:12).

Pilate heard those words with great fear. The Jews played the perfect card. They knew Pilate could not risk further conflict with Rome. If Caesar heard that Pilate was tolerating a man who challenged the authority of Rome, Caesar would remove him from office. Pilate handed Jesus over for crucifixion to save his position as governor of Judea. Of course, this was all according to God's perfect plan to redeem the world by the blood of Jesus Christ. But Pilate didn't know that. He failed to do what was right because he wanted to save his own skin.

The worst thing about compromise is that we must live with ourselves after. We may think that the compromise solves all our problems. Sometimes it does solve immediate problems. But it always leaves a pit in your stomach. I don't know if Pilate felt guilt or shame over what he did, but his strategy didn't save his position in the long run. According to Josephus, Caesar either removed Pilate as governor of Rome or did not reinstate him because Pilate had slaughtered a group of Samaritans.[2] Church historian Eusebius claimed that in AD 39, Pilate killed himself in shame.[3] Compromise always has victims. As we have seen, often the most damage is to ourselves.

## REFUSING TO COMPROMISE

Now let's look at a few Biblical characters who refused to compromise in the face of danger and persecution.

### NEHEMIAH

Nehemiah was an Israelite serving in a foreign land as cupbearer to the King of Persia. He was a man living in relative comfort in the king's palace, but he was not free. He was also dejected because his people had been exiled from their homeland. Long after the Babylonians had destroyed the temple, Nehemiah heard a report about the desolate condition of the walls of Jerusalem and was distraught. He wanted to do something. But there was risk. Looking unhappy in the presence of the king could cost him his life. Nehemiah could have compromised himself and continued to live in comfort and relative safety, but he risked those things for what he knew was right. He wanted to rebuild the city walls. He asked the king's permission to allow him to return to Israel to do it. The king allowed it and ordered his government to give Nehemiah whatever supplies he needed (Neh. 2:1-8).

More opportunities for compromise awaited Nehemiah in Jerusalem. His enemies did not want him to rebuild the city walls and gates and continually tried to stop it. As soon as he arrived, Sanballat the Horonite, Tobiah the Ammonite (2:9-10), and later, Geshem the Arab (2:19) opposed him. Nehemiah persistently rebuilt the walls when he could have compromised and opted for personal safety. Later, his enemies tried to stop the construction by physically fighting with his workers. They had to lay bricks with one hand and swing a sword with the other. Nehemiah would not stop the work. He completed the job in only fifty-two days! Nehemiah would not compromise at the expense of his own comfort, or even his own life.

### ESTHER

King Xerxes chose Esther to be Queen of Persia, but Xerxes didn't know of her Jewish descent. Haman was Xerxes second in command. Haman hated Esther's Jewish uncle Mordecai because Mordecai would not bow down to him. So Haman convinced the king that all Jews were rebellious people, a danger to the empire, and that Xerxes should exterminate them.

King Xerxes signed the edict and sealed it with his signet ring. Mordecai told Esther what had happened and begged her to speak with her husband. Esther considered compromise because she feared for her life. Not even the Queen could visit the king unless he invited her. She risked death for such a bold intrusion if he did not grant her favor. Mordecai convinced her that her position as Queen would not protect her from Xerxes' edict. He said, "For if you remain silent at this time, relief and deliverance will arise for the Jews from another place and you and your father's house will perish. And who knows whether you have not attained royalty for such a time as this?" (Esther 4:14).

Esther asked Mordecai to have all the Jews fast for the next three days, and she would do the same. She resolved that after the three days, she would visit King Xerxes, saying, "If I perish, I perish." On the third day, she called on King Xerxes and was relieved that he granted her favor to speak to him. Encouraged, she invited King Xerxes and Haman to a banquet that she prepared. When they arrived, Xerxes asked her what he could do for her. At the moment of truth, when it was time for Esther to expose Haman's plot, she didn't. There are different views as to what happened, but many agree that her courage failed. She didn't know if Xerxes would believe her, or if he would intervene for the Jews even if he did believe her. He could have ordered Esther's execution on the spot. If it's accurate to say that her courage failed, it was because she was wrestling with fear for her own life at the expense of her people. On that day, she didn't have the courage. When Xerxes asked for Esther's petition, she stammered and said, "I want you both to come back tomorrow night for another banquet that I will prepare for you."

Thankfully, she had another opportunity. The next night, she told Xerxes of Haman's plot to massacre the Jews. The King did not punish Esther, but rather, he took out his wrath on Haman. The story ends with Xerxes hanging Haman on the gallows Haman built for Mordecai, and Mordecai becoming Xerxes' number two in command. It's a fantastic story. But what if Esther continued to compromise for fear of her life? The Jews would have faced extermination. Esther may have lost her life too if Xerxes discovered her secret.

. . .

*DANIEL, SHADRACH, MESHACH, AND ABEDNEGO*

King Nebuchadnezzar was the ruler of the Babylonian empire during Babylon's exile of the southern kingdom of Judah, and for decades after. Nebuchadnezzar took the most promising young men from Judah back to Babylon. Daniel, Shadrach, Meshach, and Abednego were in their teens when Nebuchadnezzar exiled them to Babylon in about 605 B.C. Daniel 1 tells of how the young men entered a program of indoctrination into Babylonian culture, and the king's service. They would have to take new Babylonian names, learn the language and customs, eat the king's food, and drink his wine.

But Daniel would not compromise. Eating and drinking the king's food and wine would violate the law of Moses, and his conscience as a Jew. Risking his life, Daniel asked that his commander give him and his friends only vegetables for ten days. If their appearance was worse than the other young men brought into service, then he could deal with Daniel and his friends accordingly. The commander agreed. After the ten days, Daniel and his friends were in better health than the others and were vindicated.

In Daniel 3, Nebuchadnezzar built a ninety-foot golden statue for his subjects to worship every time they heard certain music playing throughout the day. Daniel himself was not present, but his other three friends were. When the music played, Shadrach, Meshach, and Abednego would not bow down. The officers brought them to the king. He offered them one more chance to bow. He said,

> "Now if you are ready, at the moment you hear the sound of the horn, flute, lyre, trigon, psaltery and bagpipe and all kinds of music, to fall down and worship the image that I have made, very well. But if you do not worship, you

will immediately be cast into the midst of a furnace of blazing fire; and what god is there who can deliver you out of my hands?" (Daniel 3:15).

They answered with one of the most amazing statements of faith and defiance in the whole Bible. They said,

"O Nebuchadnezzar, we do not need to give you an answer concerning this matter. If it be *so*, our God whom we serve is able to deliver us from the furnace of blazing fire; and He will deliver us out of your hand, O king. But *even* if *He does* not, let it be known to you, O king, that we are not going to serve your gods or worship the golden image that you have set up" (Daniel 3:16-18).

I don't know that I would have the faith and courage to take my stand before the king like they did. I pray that I would. Shadrach, Meshach and Abednego would not compromise. The king ordered the furnace heated up to seven times hotter than usual and tossed them in, but they were unharmed, because one "like a son of the gods" protected them from the flames.

By the time of Daniel 6, there was a new regime in power. The Persians had conquered Babylon, and King Darius was on the throne. The year was 539 B.C., and Daniel was in his 80's by now. He had risen high in the government because of his ability and character, which made his political enemies jealous. They convinced Darius to enact a law that anyone found praying to a god besides the king would be thrown into the lion's den. Chapter 6:1 says Daniel knew the king had signed the new law into effect. He knew of the conspiracy against him, and the consequences for disobeying the law. Daniel would not compromise. He went right on praying three times a day as was his custom.

His enemies caught Daniel praying and brought him to Darius, who was deeply distressed because of his love and respect for Daniel. But Darius had to enforce his own law. Trapped, he had Daniel thrown into the lion's den, but prayed that Daniel's God would deliver him. After a sleepless night, Darius ran down to the lion's den and was overjoyed to find that the lions had not harmed Daniel. Darius hoisted him up out of the lion's den and cast his enemies and their families in. Immediately the lions consumed them.

Daniel and his friends would not compromise their beliefs, even at the cost of their lives. Many missionaries face the same decision daily of whether to keep quiet about their beliefs or even recant their faith to save their lives. I'm sure that some have given in to the temptation to compromise in the face of death. Still, countless others have suffered martyrdom for their faith, choosing to stand firm, rather than suffering the shame of having denied Him.

## CONSEQUENCES OF COMPROMISE

Most times compromise does not achieve what we hope it will. Reuben may have had the best of intentions, but his compromise failed, because of circumstances beyond his control. Solomon compromised his morals and suffered the consequences of being married to pagan wives. Pilate's compromise left him with the shame (if he felt any) of having killed an innocent man, and he still didn't save his position. In addition to these potential consequences that could result, compromise leaves us feeling empty, because we know that we have lowered our standards for temporary pleasure or comfort, or to save our own skins.

Jesus mentioned a few other potential consequences of compromise when speaking to the churches in Asia Minor in the early chapters of Revelation.

### PERGAMUM: JESUS WOULD MAKE WAR WITH THEM (REV. 2:12-16)

Jesus rebuked the church at Pergamum because, "there were some who held to the teaching of Balaam, who kept teaching Balak to put a stumbling block before the sons of Israel, to eat things sacrificed to idols, and to commit acts of immorality." The story Jesus referenced is in Numbers chapters 22-25. But Jesus applied it to the people in the church of Pergamum that tolerated the teaching of a similar group, called the Nicolaitians. The Bible doesn't say what the specific teaching was, but most likely they were tolerating the immorality encouraged by Balaam. Jesus commanded that they repent or He would come and make war against them with the sword of His mouth.

One consequence of compromise is that false teaching, either in the church or in culture, dilutes the message of the gospel. Allowing immorality to continue in the church will result in disaster. It may have been hard for the church at Pergamum to confront the Nicolaitians. Surely, it would be much worse though for Jesus to make war against them. That was His warning to the church at Pergamum.

Jesus will discipline us if we water down or ignore His word or His teaching. That's why it's important that we never compromise doctrinal truth in our churches today.

\* \* \*

### *THYATIRA: PESTILENCE AND SICKNESS (REV 2:18-23)*

The church at Thyatira had a woman in her midst that Jesus called *Jezebel*. That may have been her actual name, but more likely it was a pseudonym for the wicked Queen Jezebel of 1 Kings. Whoever the woman was, she called herself a prophetess, and she led the people astray so that they would eat things sacrificed to idols and commit other acts of idolatry. Jesus told them that if they did not repent, He would judge and punish them for their compromise with sickness and pestilence.

### *LAODICEA: JESUS WOULD SPIT THEM OUT (REV 3:14-16)*

This church had compromised its zeal for the Lord for a life of ease. They no longer had passion for Christ. Their deeds were neither hot nor cold. They said that they were rich and needed nothing. When we compromise Jesus for the comfort of material wealth, bad results usually follow. Jesus said that because they were lukewarm, He would spit them out of His mouth. Jesus doesn't want self-satisfied, lukewarm followers. He wants people who are all-in for Him, even at considerable personal risk or cost.

## PERSONAL CONVICTION OF COMPROMISE

There are few feelings worse than conviction of sin. Sin is the result of rejecting God's standards in favor of your own. After David's affair with Bathsheba, he knew that he had compromised himself and his integrity. He had to live with that, not to mention that everyone else knew that he had done it as well. David wrote Psalm 51 in agony over his sin.

Be gracious to me, O God, according to Your lovingkindness;
According to the greatness of Your compassion blot out my
transgressions. Wash me thoroughly from my iniquity,
And cleanse me from my sin. For I know my transgressions,
And my sin is ever before me. Against You, You only, I have
sinned, And done what is evil in Your sight, So that You are
justified when You speak, And blameless when You judge
(Psalm 51:1-4).

We may feel like David every single time we compromise
our beliefs or our behavior. I don't want to feel like that.
Whatever we hoped to gain by the compromise will not be what
we had hoped, and the feeling we will have will be much worse
than we thought. I don't want to live with knowing that I have
compromised doctrinally or morally, for momentary comfort
or pleasure. It would be hard to live with the shame of denying
my Lord because I was afraid of confrontation, or even death.
It's better that we stand for what we believe in, even if it costs us
our lives, than the sickening feeling of knowing that we settled
for less than what we know is right.

## CONCLUSION

Now to finish my compromise story. After hearing the demands
of the Texas church, I asked for a meeting with the senior pastor
and the lead elder. I learned that this elder was the real power at
the church because of his deep pockets. That was just a few days
before our scheduled flight to New Jersey. The meeting didn't
happen for another day or two, and by then, I finally recognized
the red flags I should have seen all along. I went into the
meeting with the mindset that I would not pastor at this church
at any salary. But I did want to understand their thinking.

At the meeting, I expressed my disbelief that they would hold me hostage like that, and that they would not allow me to fulfill my obligation to the New Jersey church. From their perspective, they wanted me to accept their offer before I left, to prove that they were my first choice, I suppose. I thought it was unethical to commit to them before seeing through my obligation at the New Jersey church. Then they suggested that perhaps I was not the right candidate for the position.

From my perspective, the way they conducted the entire process should have caused concern for me a lot earlier. I just ignored the obvious issues because I was desperate for a pastoral position. I was tempted to compromise. Molly told me consistently that the Texas church was not right for us. They had little concern about our personal or financial needs. In fact, when they were considering my salary, they made us submit our detailed monthly budget. We had to list everything from home expenses to our budget for dog food. We had nothing to hide, but still, we felt naked and exposed on a spreadsheet. Then they flippantly told us that we needed to learn to live on less. They also strongly hinted that they didn't want Molly to get a job to help support us because the church needed her to serve too. It was obvious that they were trying to get a two-for-one deal. It was demeaning.

In addition, they had a quota of hours that I would have to work. Then they demanded that I add 10% to the hourly quota as a tithe of my time. Now, I'm not afraid of hard work. I've been self-employed for most of my life and have put in some very long days and weeks. And now that I'm a pastor, I never stop working. But these demands made me feel like a teenager interviewing for an entry-level hourly position at a fast-food restaurant. "You want fries with that?" Before I stepped foot in the church, they were planning to micromanage every minute of my time. I told them thanks, but no thanks.

That Friday, my family boarded a plane to New Jersey. We had an exciting time preaching in that church and meeting the people. They were lovely and hospitable. After numerous interviews, our family was invited back to the church for a question and answer session with the entire congregation. Molly and I sat on the platform while our two children were in one of the front pews. The elders invited members of the church to ask us questions. We had no idea what people would ask, but we felt at ease when the subjects ranged from how Molly and I met, to our salvation stories, and even our interests and hobbies. The meeting went way longer than planned.

At the very end, one of the elders of the church stood up and grabbed the microphone. He said, "I promised myself that I would always ask this question," and then asked me my position on drinking alcohol. I knew that he expected, or at least hoped, that I would denounce the use of alcohol. I delicately responded that the Bible doesn't prohibit the use of alcohol, but it does prohibit drunkenness, and I supported it with Scripture. I told him that I believe that Christians have liberty in that area, but that we should never be a stumbling block to others.

He did not like that answer and continued to challenge me in front of my wife, my kids and the whole congregation. I did not change my belief just because he didn't like it. Then he made a big mistake. With my kids in the room, he asked, "What if you allow your kids to drink alcohol, and after the first taste, they become alcoholics?" Well, Mama Bear Molly didn't like that question too much. She took the microphone from me and with all the restraint she could muster, informed him that she was a child of an alcoholic father. She knew perfectly well the dangers of alcohol abuse and wasn't planning to introduce our kids to alcohol. That ended the exchange, but we were both somewhat rattled.

We went back to Texas, and the chairman of the search committee called me soon after. He apologized for what happened. The entire congregation was surprised by the question and the lack of grace given by that elder after my answer. He also told me that they had asked that elder to step down. They offered me the senior pastor position soon after. I was wary, but other than that one exchange, I really liked the opportunity and the people. Plus, I was desperate for a pastor position, even though I knew that my family didn't want to move again.

I eventually agreed with Molly that all things considered, this was not the right church for us either. The phone call declining the position was one of the hardest I ever had to make. I felt terrible for myself because I had just missed out on two opportunities with nothing else on the horizon. I felt awful for them because they had invested so much time, money, and effort in us. We realized that our kids had settled in and were happy in Texas. After four years of living here, we—or maybe just I—never really considered how hard it would be for them if we pulled up our stakes again.

I had two chances to compromise. I could have canceled my preaching engagement with the New Jersey church, and accepted the Texas church's offer. Or, I could have accepted the New Jersey church's offer and moved for the sake of having a job, over what was best for my family. I am so thankful for God's (and Molly's!) guidance over those months. As I was saying, "no" to both churches, God was preparing the right position for me. However, before I would be ready for it, I had to wrap up my law firm, which was still ongoing. I also had to get healthier mentally, as all of this was happening during my struggles with anxiety and depression. It took two more years until I was ready.

The apostle John wrote, "Do not love the world or the things in the world" (1 John 2:15 ESV). When we do, we are likely to compromise. Sometimes when we are wavering, God tickles us with a feather to get our attention. If that doesn't work, He might have to hit us in the head with a hammer. That's what happened to me. He had to make it so clear that what I was about to do would be disastrous, and finally, I listened. Compromise may get us what we want short term, but the bill always comes due. Always.

There's a hymn by Haldor Lillenas written in 1913 called "No Compromise." It's a perfect summary of what our position should be toward compromise.

Verse 1:
No compromise with evil
Shall be our battle cry,
For God and right must conquer,
And sin and wrong must die;

Unflinching we are standing,
Uncompromisingly,
Beneath the flag of holiness
Forever we will be.

Refrain:
No compromise, no compromise,
This shall be our battle cry,
For God and right we will boldly fight,
We will keep the standard high.

Verse 2:

No compromise with error,
For Bible truth we stand,
Let none remove the landmarks
Erected by God's hand

With loyalty our watchword
And faith in Christ our stay,
We'll bravely storm the forts of sin
And thro' Him win the day.

Verse 3:

No compromise with worldliness,
No yielding to the wrong,
No lowering the standard
That's stood thro' ages long;
With Jesus as our leader,
His Spirit as our guide,
We'll firmly stand for righteousness
Whatever may betide.[4]

# EPILOGUE

Since you've read this far, you probably realize at least two things. 1) Your author is a very imperfect person; and 2) Jesus is bigger than our worst failures, our biggest mistakes, our greatest temptations, and our heaviest burdens. God loves imperfect people (That's the only kind there are!) and His love conquers over all things. I have used Biblical examples in each chapter to show that God uses ordinary, flawed, sinful people to achieve His purposes, and to show that there is no one beyond His redemption. There is no situation so bad that He can't make beauty from it.

I have used stories from my own life to show the same thing. God used some of these events to draw me to Him when I was an unbeliever. Now that I'm a believer, he used other events to help grow me closer to the person He wants me to be. The Christian life is a life of growth, and sometimes it's marked by two steps forward and one step back, sometimes one step forward and two steps back! God is sovereign over it all. He has been ever-present in my life, both before and after I was aware of it, to take what could have been ugly and use it for good.

That's not to say that our foibles won't result in God's discipline. Sometimes they will. But God disciplines those whom He loves, to achieve His purposes.

I have enjoyed writing this book. The two most difficult things have been first, to limit the subjects to only ten. They best fit the overall theme of how we face life's challenges. I have a list of topics yet to write about that's much longer than what I've included here. Maybe those topics will find their way someday into a second book about how we face life's successes head on. We face as much adversity in our successes as in our failures.

The second challenge has been exposing personal stories that are very embarrassing to me. I've done and thought a lot of foolish things. But if the result is that I have pointed you to Jesus so that you see His beauty, majesty, and grace, and that you have learned how to face your own challenges head on, then I would consider this project a success.

* * *

IF THIS BOOK HELPED YOU AND YOU BELIEVE THAT OTHERS COULD benefit from it too, I would greatly appreciate it if you would leave a brief review wherever you buy books. Thank you in advance!

* * *

TYPE THIS URL TO DOWNLOAD MY FREE EBOOK:
https://dl.bookfunnel.com/usje1pnyu0
This Is God's Plan?! How We Can Be Certain in Days of Uncertainty

. . .

**ALSO AVAILABLE WHERE BOOKS ARE SOLD**

God Is Everywhere! Recognizing Our Extraordinary God in Ordinary Life

You can connect with me on Facebook at Facebook.com/ BobJennerich, and Twitter.com/bob_jennerich. Go to BobJennerich.com read my blog and listen to sermons I delivered at Grace Redeemer Community Church, Garland, TX.

## OTHER BOOKS BY THE AUTHOR

**Type this Url to Download My Free Ebook:**

https://dl.bookfunnel.com/usje1pnyu0

This Is God's Plan?! How We Can Be Certain in Days of Uncertainty

**Also available where books are sold**

God Is Everywhere! Recognizing Our Extraordinary God in Ordinary Life

# NOTES

## 1. ANXIETY

1. Sheryl Ankrom, "The Difference Between Fear and Anxiety," accessed November 16, 2020, https://www.verywellmind.com/fear-and-anxiety-differences-and-similarities-2584399.
2. Calvin, J., & Pringle, J. (2010). *Commentaries on the Epistles of Paul the Apostle to the Corinthians* (Vol. 2, p. 118). Bellingham, WA: Logos Bible Software.
3. Johnson Oatman, Jr. "Count Your Blessings," (1897), Hymnary.org, accessed November 16, 2020, https://hymnary.org/text/when_upon_lifes_billows_you_are_tempest.
4. William Cowper, "God Moves in a Mysterious Way," (1774), from a poem by Cowper called "Light Shining Out of Darkness," Hymnary.org, accessed November 16, 2020, https://hymnary.org/text/god_moves_in_a_mysterious_way.

## 2. FEAR

1. Timothy Keller, *Prayer: Experiencing Awe and Intimacy with God*, (New York: Penguin Books, 2014), 228.
2. John Newton, "Amazing Grace," (1779), Hymnary.org, accessed November 16, 2020, https://hymnary.org/text/amazing_grace_how_sweet_the_sound.

## 3. DOUBT

1. Oswald Chambers, *The Quotable Oswald Chambers*, (2011), accessed November 16, 2020, https://libquotes.com/search/?q=doubt+oswald+chambers.
2. Henry Drummond, *The Greatest Thing in the World and Other Addresses*, (New York: James Pott & Co., 1890), 92.
3. John MacArthur, *Solving the Problem of Doubt*, September 6, 1981. Grace Community Church, accessed November 16, 2020, https://www.gty.org/library/sermons-library/2285/solving-the-problem-of-doubt.

4. Albert B. Simpson, "Settle it Today," accessed September 8, 2020, https://hymnary.org/text/o_struggling_doubting_christian.

## 4. REJECTION

1. James A. Brooks, Mark, General Editor, David S. Dockery, Vol. 23, New American Commentary, (Nashville: Broadman & Holman Publishers, 1992), 98.
2. John Bakewell, "Hail, Thou Once-Despised Jesus!," (1757), Hymnary.org, accessed     November     16,     2020,     https://hymnary.org/text/hail_thou_once_despised_jesus.

## 5. TEMPTATION

1. Martin Luther, "Quotes," accessed 8/29/20, https://www.goodreads.com/quotes/757798-you-cannot-keep-birds-from-flying-over-your-head-but
2. William G.T. Shedd, *Dogmatic Theology* (New York: Scribner, 1891), 2:336
3. Charles C. Ryrie, *Basic Theology*, (Chicago: Moody Publishers, 1986), 305.
4. Thomas Lea, *Hebrews, James,* Holman New Testament Commentary, gen ed. Max Anders, vol. 10, (Nashville, TN: Broadman & Holman Publishers, 1999), 74.
5. Annie S. Hawks, Robert Lowry, "I Need Thee Every Hour," (1872), Hymnary.org, accessed November 16, 2020, https://hymnary.org/text/i_need_thee_every_hour_most_gracious_lor.

## 6. GUILT AND SHAME

1. Walter Bauer, *A Greek-English Lexicon of the New Testament and other Early Christian Literature*, Revised and edited by Frederick W. Danker, 3rd ed. Chicago: University of Chicago Press, 2000.
2. Elvina M. Hall, "Jesus Paid it All," (1865), Hymnary.org, accessed November 17,                    2020,                    https://hymnary.org/text/i_hear_the_savior_say_thy_strength_indee.

## 7. MONEY

1. Walter Bauer. *A Greek-English Lexicon of the New Testament and other Early Christian Literature*, Revised and edited by Frederick W. Danker, 3rd ed. Chicago: University of Chicago Press, 2000.
2. "Be Thou My Vision." Eleanor Henrietta Hull, Mary Elizabeth Byrne, Hymnary.org, accessed November 17, 2020, https://hymnary.org/text/be_thou_my_vision_o_lord_of_my_heart

## 8. COMPARISON

1. In other epistles, Paul did have to assert his apostleship and authority at times (see Galatians 1), not to exalt himself, but to prove to his readers that Jesus called him as a true apostle with authority, and commissioned him to preach the gospel.
2. Gottfried Arnold, "Bliss Beyond Compare," Hymnary.org, accessed November 17, 2020, https://hymnary.org/text/bliss_beyond_compare.

## 9. SICKNESS

1. Josephus, *Antiquities of the Jews*, 18.4.1-2.
2. Victor P. Hamilton, *Handbook on the Pentateuch*, (Grand Rapids, MI: Baker Books, 2005), 255-256.
3. John Piper, "Is God an Egomaniac?," (audio recording, 2013) , accessed November 17, 2020, https://www.desiringgod.org/interviews/is-god-an-egomaniac.
4. Augustus Montague Toplady, "Rock of Ages," (1776), Hymnary.org, accessed November 17, 2020, https://hymnary.org/text/rock_of_ages_cleft_for_me_let_me_hide.

## 10. COMPROMISE

1. "Compromise," Miriam-Webster Online Dictionary, accessed November 18, 2020, https://www.merriam-webster.com/dictionary/compromise.
2. Josephus, *Antiquities of the Jews*, 18.4.1-2.
3. Eusebius, *Church History*, 2.6.7.
4. Haldor Lillenas, "No Compromise," (1913), Hymnary.org, accessed November 18, 2020, https://hymnary.org/text/no_compromise_with_evil_shall_be_our_bat.

# BIBLIOGRAPHY

Ankrom, Sheryl. "The Difference Between Fear and Anxiety." Accessed November 18, 2020. https://www.verywell-mind.com/fear-and-anxiety-differences-and-similarities-2584399.

Arnold, Gottfried. "Bliss Beyond Compare." 1666-1714, Moravian Book of Worship #594. Accessed November 18, 2020. https://hymnary.org/text/bliss_beyond_compare.

Bakewell, John. "Hail, Thou Once Despised Jesus," 1757. Accessed November 18, 2020. https://hymnary.org/text/hail_thou_once_despised_jesus.

Bauer, Walter. *A Greek-English Lexicon of the New Testament and other Early Christian Literature*. Revised and edited by Frederick W. Danker, 3rd ed. Chicago: University of Chicago Press, 2000.

Brooks, James A. *Mark*. General Editor, David S. Dockery, Vol. 23, New American Commentary. Nashville: Broadman & Holman Publishers, 1992.

Calvin, John. *Commentaries on the Epistles of Paul the Apostle to the Corinthians.* Vol. 2, 1546. Translated by Pringle, John, 1848. Bellingham, WA: Logos Bible Software. 2010.

Chambers, Oswald. *The Quotable Oswald Chambers*. Compiled and edited by David McCasland: Grand Rapids, MI: Discovery House, 2011. Accessed September 8,2020. https://libquotes.-com/search/?q=doubt+oswald+chambers.

Cowper, William. "God Moves in a Mysterious Way," from a poem by Cowper called "Light Shining Out of Darkness," 1773. Accessed November 18, 2020. https://hymnary.org/text/god_moves_in_a_mysterious_way.

Drummond, Henry. *The Greatest Thing in the World and Other Addresses*. New York: James Pott & Co., 1890.

Eusebius. *Church History.*

Hall, Elvina M. "Jesus Paid it All," 1865. Accessed November 18, 2020. https://hymnary.org/text/i_hear_the_sav-ior_say_thy_strength_indee.

Hamilton, Victor P. *Handbook on the Pentateuch*: Grand Rapids, MI: Baker Books, 2005.

Hawks, Annie S. and Lowry, Robert. "I Need Thee Every Hour," 1872. Accessed November 18, 2020.

https://hymnary.org/text/i_need_thee_every_hour_most_-gracious_lor.

Hull, Eleanor Henrietta and Byrne, Mary Elizabeth. "Be Thou My Vision," 1912. Accessed November 18, 2020, https://hymnary.org/text/be_thou_my_vision_o_lord_of_my_heart.

Josephus. *Antiquities of the Jews.*

Keller, Timothy. *Prayer: Experiencing Awe and Intimacy with God.* Penguin Books: New York, NY, 2014.

Lea, Thomas. *Hebrews, James.* Holman New Testament Commentary, General Editor, Max Anders vol. 10. Nashville, TN: Broadman & Holman Publishers, 1999.

Lillenas, Haldor. "No Compromise," 1913. Accessed November 18, 2020. https://hymnary.org/text/no_compromise_with_-_evil_shall_be_our_bat.

Luther, Martin. Accessed November 18, 2020. https://www.-goodreads.com/quotes/757798-you-cannot-keep-birds-from-flying-over-your-head-but.

MacArthur, John. "Solving the Problem of Doubt." September 6, 1981. Grace Community Church, https://www.gty.org/library/sermons-library/2285/solving-the-problem-of-doubt.

Merriam-Webster.com. "Compromise." https://www.merriam-webster.com/dictionary/compromise. Accessed 10/25/20.

Newton, John. "Amazing Grace," 1772. Accessed November 18, 2020,
https://hymnary.org/text/amazing_grace_how_sweet_the_sound

Oatman, Jr., Johnson. "Count Your Blessings," 1897. Accessed November 18, 2020. https://hymnary.org/text/when_upon_lifes_billows_y-ou_are_tempest.

Piper, John. "Is God an Egomaniac?" Accessed November 18, 2020. https://www.desiringgod.org/interviews/is-god-an-egomaniac.

Ryrie, Charles C. *Basic Theology*: Chicago: Moody Publishers, 1986.

Shedd, William G.T. *Dogmatic Theology*: New York: Scribner, 1891.

Simpson, Albert B. *Settle it Today*. Accessed September 8, 2020. https://hymnary.org/text/o_struggling_doubting_christian.

Toplady, Augustus Montague. "Rock of Ages," 1776. Accessed November 18, 2020. https://hymnary.org/text/rock_of_ages_-cleft_for_me_let_me_hide.

# ABOUT THE AUTHOR

Bob Jennerich was a lawyer in a small law firm in New Jersey when he became a Christian. In 2011, he and his wife, Molly, and their two children, Allison and Brian sold their home in New Jersey and moved to Texas so Bob could attend Dallas Theological Seminary. He accepted the call to become Senior Pastor of Grace Redeemer Community Church in Garland, Texas, in July 2017. Every Sunday he preaches the same gospel that he rejected for so many years. He jokes that if you would have told him 20 years ago that he would be pastoring a church in Texas today, he would have thought that you were crazy.

Bob's passion is to read and study the Bible and teach it to others, so that they too may experience the life transformation that happens when people receive the gospel. The inspiration to write books sprung from his passion to spread the gospel beyond the walls of the church he pastors.

Bob also loves to travel and exercise. He's finished 12 marathons. He's a sports fan, but mostly from the bleachers these days. One of his goals is to go to a game in every major league baseball stadium.